Life's Too Short To Drink Cheap Wine

Kerry Smithers

Copyright © 2010 Kerry Smithers

All rights reserved.

ISBN: 1466273909
ISBN-13: 9781466273900

DEDICATION

For my beautiful Trinity..

Intro

No matter how well you know somebody, you can never be sure that there aren't some surprises left. It's easy to think that the part of a person you see, the face that is turned toward you, tells you about the rest; that, like a hologram, every section contains the whole. I think it just doesn't turn out that way, though, no matter how good a view you had.

I knew Will Smithers, my husband, as well as anyone knew him. We were constant companions, living together, working and playing together, almost from the time we met. When Will died--abruptly, unfairly, incomprehensibly--at the age of 35, I thought I knew who it was that I had lost. We had been together for ten years full of surprises and adventures, but I never suspected that even after the worst day of my life, November 8, 2002, when Will got into his newest toy, a Gazelle helicopter, at the

McArthur airport on Long Island, and was never seen again, he wasn't done surprising me.

Do you remember the movie *Paper Moon*, with Ryan and Tatum O'Neill? Ryan O'Neill was a con artist, and one of his scams was to go to the homes of the recently deceased and tell the widow that her husband had ordered a bible inscribed for her, but there was still money due. He would walk away with five or ten dollars for a fifty cent bible. Well, about two weeks after Will's death, I got a phone call from a warehouse in Kennebunk, Maine.

We're sorry for your loss, they say, but Will Smithers has an electron microscope in storage here. If this was a scam, it was a much more profitable one that Ryan O'Neill's; electron microscopes can cost as much as hundreds of thousands of dollars. It wasn't a scam, though. Will had bought it on eBay; he'd never taken delivery, but it was already paid for.

Will never would have admitted it, but he didn't have a formal background in science, or even a college degree, but after ten years I knew that didn't stop him once something caught his attention. It hadn't stopped him from designing Z-Plan, software for SCUBA rebreathers that became one of the standards for the most dangerous kind of technical diving, where one miscalculation can cost your life; and it hadn't stopped him from tinkering with atomic clock design—there were three or four in the house when he died. Will was like that—he was completely self-taught, and the most brilliant person I have ever known. He was a genuine renaissance man; once a topic caught his interest, it wasn't long before he could talk about it on a Ph. D. level

Toward the end, he was reading a lot about genetic engineering. It sounds ridiculous, but when Will first said that he wanted to clone himself, even though I joked about it (I asked him to at least practice by cloning our cat, Zach, first), I knew enough to take him seriously.

So, while buying a multi-hundred thousand dollar electron microscope on eBay the way somebody else might buy an extra laptop battery, it wasn't out of character for Will.

No problem, I tell the guy, my father-in-law lives up there I'll just have him swing by and pick it up.

Lady, I don't think you understand. It's the size of a desk and weighs a thousand pounds. You need a truck.

Oh.

So, I sent out an email to my friends: "I find that I am in possession of an electron microscope, and I don't really feel I have a need for one. It's a thousand pounds and the size of a desk. Does anyone have a favorite university that I can make a gift of this to?" That was my immediate reaction, because I thought Will would have loved to just donate it where it would do some good.

Eventually Cody Callihan, a Tradeware employee who worked very closely with Will and me, told me that he knew someone in the anthropology department at the University of Florida, his girlfriend's brother, and as soon as they heard, they were all over it. Cody didn't realize it at the time, but the University of Florida is where I went to school. Done! I said.

So I made it a gift to the University of Florida and had it trucked down. I told them that I didn't know if it worked, I didn't know anything about it, but they were very happy to take it off my hands. They got in touch with the manufacturer and had them come in to set it up and train some of their people, and then they invited me down for a dedication ceremony. I was happy to go, but I put it off until fall (so I could catch the U.F. Gators in a football game).

So October 2003, coming up on the anniversary of Will's death, I went down to Gainesville, and it was absolutely fascinating. The entire anthropology department was just ecstatic to have it. They were now the only university in the Southeast with one of these. The whole time I was there, they were saying, Kerry, you have no idea how much this helps us; we can attract professors, we can attract students. It also obviously meant funding.

They had a cocktail party for me (I think I surprised them; they were expecting some elderly blue-haired lady and got me instead), but before that we did a tour of the whole anthropology department. I saw the lab with the plaque outside that read *The William Smithers Scanning Electron Microscope Lab*, and inside was another sign with both our names on it. We went into each of the other labs, and they had arranged for Ph.D. students to present demonstrations of everything. It was all going over my head, of course, but I thought, Oh, my god, Will would have so loved this. That's when I realized what the labs reminded me of. They looked just like Will's workshop in our house. He was constantly working on some technical project, as a hobby.

But here's the thing. A little while before I went down to Florida, I got a call from Morgain Harris, in Seattle. Morgain and Will had never met, but they had worked together designing a rebreather, and Will talked to him on the phone every day. I got used to picking up the phone and hearing "This is Morgain. Where's Will?" Morgain told me that even though they'd never met, he felt he knew Will really well, and was very upset by his death.

(Actually, "Where's Will," was one of the themes of my life with him, since half the time he wouldn't answer the phone, and he flatly refused to install an answering machine. He felt it was an imposition when somebody left a message, because then you were obliged to return the call. If you just let the phone rang until the caller gave up, they'd try again later, and the responsibility remained where it belonged, which you can't really argue with. Anyway, people didn't say "Hello" to me; they said "Where's Will?")

I hadn't heard from Morgain in some time, so when he asked me, What are you going to with the scanning electron microscope? I said, What do you mean? I already gave it to the University of Florida.

No, it's here in Seattle, Morgan said.

What?

Sorry, but yeah, it's right here.

Will, it turned out, had bought *two* electron microscopes on eBay.

I told Morgain I was going to pretend I hadn't heard anything about it, but he needed it out of his shop. It's in storage now, until I can find another school to give it to.

Chapter One

Kerry and Will

I have never been much of a writer and never really felt the need to write anything down, but I decided that I wanted to write about Will, to set him down on paper as best I could. I wanted our daughter, Trinity, only three when he died, to know him as much as she could, to hear all the stories, and have them written down in a book so she can turn to them again when she's older, when perhaps I myself won't remember them as well. (Yes, she was named after *that* Trinity, the Carrie Ann Moss, *Matrix*, Trinity, or at least that's what I was thinking. Will, well, we'll get to that later.) But I wanted others to read about him, too.

It felt like a story that had to be told, that people would want to read. Even allowing for my obvious bias, Will was the most interesting man I've ever known, and I knew other people would find his story fascinating.

Very early in our relationship, Will asked me if I would like to go on an adventure with him. Thank God I had the guts to say "Yes!"

***

In 1992, at the time I met Will, I was married to a nice guy and we had a pretty nice life. We were living in nice little condo in Quincy, just outside of Boston. There was nothing exceptional about me, and really, there never had been, and I had always been fine with that. I assumed — or would have assumed, if I'd stopped to think about it — that that's how things were always going to be.

I'd met my husband, Daryl, while I was in college, in Gainesville. He wasn't a student there It was my junior year, and I was living off-campus in a house with four roommates; one of them worked as a bartender, and I met Daryl through her. We became friends, and then best friends. It was that sort of relationship, but I thought I was in love. I thought this was what they meant when they talked about meeting the right guy, so when Daryl eventually asked me to marry him, I did.

He was working as a cook at the time, and when I graduated, we moved back up to Boston, where I'd grown up. We were together seven years, and I put him through chef school, and by this time, he had a good job working in the corporate cafeteria at Houghton Mifflin. I didn't notice that it was okay with me that our working hours didn't leave us much time together. What finally got my attention was when Daryl decided it was time to have a family. I just wasn't ready to do that. I couldn't imagine how people managed a job and children, but even if it wasn't for that, something inside me told me that this wasn't the right thing to do.

I guess that instead of facing what was going on at home, questioning how we got to the point where we wanted such different things, I decided that what was wrong with my life was work. Though I loved programming, I was growing bored with my job at Belvedere Financial Systems; I wasn't being challenged. So I stayed on the pill without telling Daryl, and started sending out resumes to agencies.

There were lots of jobs for programmers then, and I'd been to a few interviews when I got a call for a job that sounded perfect. In a new suit from Ann Taylor, I showed up at Thomson Financial Networks for my interview. It seemed like a great place to work. The offices were located in Boston near the bay, in beautifully renovated old brick buildings. I got off the T (which is the subway in Boston) at South Station, and walked over the bridge by the re-creation of the ship where the Boston Tea Party took place, and down Congress Street.

When I arrived, I was escorted to a manager's office. The interview with Stan seemed to go pretty well. My skills and experience seemed to be what they were looking for. They were putting together two teams of developers, each focused on a new product, to build a brand new system from scratch. This was exactly the type of thing I wanted to hear--I like creating new software and had no interest in getting a new job where I'd end up maintaining or testing software built by someone else.

Suddenly, the manager excused himself and left me alone in his office. He was gone for a few minutes, and when he came back he offered me a job. I was very surprised; this is not how things usually go in my industry. There's always some discussion in-house after you leave, and usually they'll call around to make some inquiries too; days can pass before you actually get an offer.

Much later, I was to find out that this was the first time Will Smithers changed the direction of my life. He'd been listening in to the meeting, and when Stan left the office, it was to find out what Will thought of me. He told Stan to hire me on the spot.

It would actually be a bit of a pay cut from my job at Belvedere, but I accepted immediately. I was more interested in the right type of job then the size of the paycheck, and this was exactly the kind of job I was hoping for. After calling Daryl, I just about ran back to my current job and gave them my two weeks notice.

***

When I started my new job at Thomson, I joined about twenty people that had been assembled for the project, but my team was small, just me and two other developers. At first, they didn't even have computers for us to work on, so we just had a lot of meetings where management told us what we were going to be doing once we did have computers. My team would be working on an order-routing system for stock trading.

Back then, most companies still weren't transmitting their trade orders electronically, and the ones that did didn't have a common system they could use to put their orders into the brokerage houses. So, if you were an institution that wanted to start doing electronic trading through six different brokers, you'd have to hire developers to create six different interfaces that could talk to the proprietary software at each of the brokerage houses. It was as if you had to install six entirely separate intercom systems, each wired differently, one to each firm you did business with, instead of just having a phone installed so that you could pick it up and call whoever you wanted to.

What we were setting out to do was create the equivalent of a telephone switchboard system. It would be a set of high-powered servers hosting software that let people enter their trade orders into a graphical user interface at one end, which would be routed to the right broker at the other end. Ideally, it would be as simple and transparent as sending an email through AOL (but without the spam; this was a closed, private system, and nothing got on it that wasn't supposed to be there).

But, really, all you need to remember is that this was a medium-sized, high-tech company in the early nineties, which contained a lot of young people making good money by doing interesting technical things.

A few days after I'd started, there was a new person at one of the big meetings. He was a young, good-looking guy in an expensive suit, and it was immediately clear to me that he was extremely smart. There was something about him. Even before he was introduced, you could tell that everybody in the room was paying attention to him. He had that kind of charisma. Stan introduced him as Will Smithers, and explained that he'd be providing an API, the application programming interface. This was going to be used to handle the interprocess communications for the system. It's what would let one application talk to and interact with another. An API is what lets you take a picture you took with your digital camera and drop it right into a Word document, or a steaming video file onto a web page. Thomson's trading system would consist of many applications and for everything to work, there had to be a mechanism running to make sure they could all communicate with one another.

Will took over the meeting and began to explain the proposed system. He talked easily about complex technical details, illustrating them by drawing all sorts of diagrams. I have to admit that I was a bit lost before long, but he gave us so much information so quickly that I really don't think I was the only one in the room who was confused. He finished up by handing out a thirty-page white paper on the design and implementation of the system, and asked us to read it for tomorrow's meeting.

We all went home and read it, and the next day everybody had lots of questions. Will easily answered them, but somehow, when he was done, it still wasn't exactly clear to me how any of this was going to work.

***

We finally got our computers, Sun Sparc workstations, a couple of days after that (they sat in boxes against a wall until I took one and set it up; the other developers got very upset and insisted that I should wait for somebody from the IT department to come by and do it, but nobody ever did, and when they all saw me sitting there happily tapping away on my new computer, they finally followed suit—one of the advantages of having worked for small companies is that I'm used to doing a lot of things for myself), but there wasn't really a lot we could do.

Time went by—weeks, then months—and I knew that we were waiting for software from Will, but I still wasn't quite sure how he fit into the structure of the company. As far as I could tell, he didn't actually work for Thomson. I got the sense that he lived in New York City, and he'd fly in sporadically to have meetings with management. I couldn't tell how old he was either. He seemed too young to have the foundations of a project of this magnitude resting on his shoulders—at one point, a few months in, I heard Helen, one of the managers, yell, "We're betting our whole trading system on some guy who's younger than my paper boy?" On the other hand, he always looked the part, dressed in designer suits, with his hair slicked back like some power player in a movie.

Usually I could tell where a person fit into the business; whether somebody really was a player or just a bullshitter, but Will had me completely stumped. Months were going by and still no product from Will. It was hard not to conclude that he'd sold Thomson vaporware — a euphemism for software that you've sold to someone, even though it doesn't actually exist .

On a personal level, I thought he was very attractive, but honestly, his intensity scared me. And of course, I was a married woman, so I wasn't even thinking in that direction.

***

One day, I was in my cube, minding my own business, debugging some unimportant piece of code — make-work, really — when Will quietly walked up to me and said, "Hi, I'm Will, your debugging friend!"

I just stared at him. He made me nervous. Why did he say that?

"What are you working on?"

"Nothing, really. I'm just trying to learn some things to get ready to write the code when we get your stuff."

"Do you have the Stevens book?"

"No."

"Oh, you have to get it! It's the bible. No, wait, I have a copy—I'll give it to you!"

I don't know if I can convey this, but he was as excited about me—someone he barely knew—learning sockets in C (don't worry, you don't need to know), as most people would be about, well, maybe not winning the lottery, but close to it. He was incredibly full of life. I'd had one conversation with him, and I already knew that I'd never met anyone like him.

That night, I was home with Daryl, watching TV, and a commercial for David Letterman came on.

"Hi, I'm Dave, your late-night friend," he said in the commercial, and I burst out laughing, finally getting the joke Will had made seven hours earlier.

Daryl wondered what I thought was so funny, and I told him the story, but he didn't find it very amusing.

***

Over the next month or so, Will would pop in here and there and promise everyone that the API was almost ready. Having broken the ice, we started talking to each other regularly, and we developed a friendly rapport. He told me that he had worked as a consultant on Wall Street for years, and had recently started his own company, Financial Technology Corp. He had a few clients in Manhattan and now he'd sold this product to Thomson. So, now I knew where he fit in, and I was pretty amazed that he was doing all this, especially when I found out he was only twenty-five.

Around this point, going on about four months since I'd been hired and the project started, Thomson moved to new offices. That's when I started giving Will a hard time, kidding around and telling him he better deliver something soon. People really were getting anxious. We'd had time to change offices, and we still hadn't seen a single line of code from him. I was pretty content, myself; I was learning new things, and getting ready by writing apps for practice, even though I knew I'd have to throw them out and start all over once we got Will's system. But one developer had already moved to another project, and the one that was left just sort of sat around all day waiting for someone to tell him what to do. It wasn't going unnoticed by the higher-ups.

Then Will disappeared for about two weeks.

I remembered he'd told me that he'd taken an apartment in Back Bay, so I'd thought I'd be seeing more of him, but nobody saw him at all until one day he walked into the office looking like hell. He had big dark circles under his eyes, and instead of the usual designer suit, he was in jeans and an old T-shirt.

He walked up to my cubicle, smiled, and slapped a quarter-inch tape down on my desk.

I didn't say a word. I picked up the tape, inserted it into the tape drive of my computer, and typed the command to extract the contents. Screen after screen of code filled my monitor—there was an incredible amount of code on the tape.

I looked up at him. "You wrote this in the last two weeks, didn't you?"

He smiled, held his finger up to his mouth and said, "Don't tell anyone." He confessed to me then that he'd sold Thomson vaporware, but finally they were putting so much pressure on him that he secluded himself in the tiny apartment to crank out product, holed up with a laptop, a milk crate for a desk, and a futon on the floor. Every day, he woke up, ran a couple of miles, and then went back to the apartment and coded until he had to sleep again. When he remembered, he'd call out for some food. In two weeks, he had accomplished what everybody thought he'd been working on for four months.

Well, now it was my job to learn what he'd written, and I got to work. What happened next is pretty embarrassing, because it's probably the nerdiest instance of falling in love in history. As I read his code I found myself inside his head, seeing how he thought, and he was brilliant. The code was so elegant, so well thought-out, that I couldn't believe anybody could have done it in two weeks. Sometimes, I'd come across something in the structure that was so surprising that I'd laugh out loud.

We founded Tradeware not long after that; it was built around that same code, and it's a thirty million dollar company now. Will wrote that code over ten years ago, which in the programming world isn't just a lifetime, it's multiple generations, and we're still using it. He had written the basic building blocks of the trading system running here today, and when new people come into the company and see it, they're still impressed. The programmers starting out today might be too young to know who the Beatles are, but they're still in awe of Will's code.

Will started flying back and forth from New York to Boston more, and he was around a lot so we could talk about the project, and what was going to happen next. We were spending a lot more time together, and it wasn't all business. He was extremely funny and had all these wild stories about his travels and business struggles. He'd been all over—he'd lived in California and Colorado, and traveled to exotic spots like Grand Cayman to go scuba diving. He told me how great the Hotel Bora-Bora was and how beautiful the Mauna Lani Bay in Hawaii was, and he kept on saying things like "We have to go there."

One day, management called a meeting of everyone involved in the project to discuss how things were proceeding. At this point, of the twenty-five people assembled, Will and I were the only ones working on my end of things. We needed to give them and overview of our progress and designs, and Will made the presentation. He was great at this sort of thing, and he was even better at it when discussing an actual product, instead of vaporware. I can still remember sitting there, watching him in front of the white board again, drawing diagrams and shooting ideas out into the room a mile a minute, when suddenly I thought, clear as a bell, "I am completed fucked!"

I realized at that moment that I was head-over-heels in love with this guy. I couldn't concentrate on what Will was saying; all I could think about was how to deal with the problem of being married to one man and in love with another.

***

Right around then, management gave Will an office, down the hall from me, and from then on, he was in every day. One morning, I came in at nine, as usual, and walked down to Will's office to say hello. I looked in the window and he wasn't there, so I went in to leave a note on his desk. I looked down and there was Will, sleeping under the desk with a little pillow. He was living in the office.

I let him sleep, but later I went back. "If you're going to sleep under your desk, Will, you should wake up before everyone's here."

That's when we really started getting close, because he opened up to me. The fact was, he put on a great show, but he had no money. He was living hand to mouth. He'd get a big check from a client, spend it all, and then scrape by until the next one came in.

The apartment in Back Bay had only been rented for a month, and he had to give up the little studio apartment he was renting on Pearl Street in New York; they'd turned off the electricity a while ago, and he had been running his hot plate and computer off electricity he pirated from the hallway, living on a bag of rice.

I started spending more and more time with him. We would go out with a bunch of people from the office almost every night after work, to a little Chinese restaurant nearby — the food was terrible, but it was close, and we were usually just drinking — and stay for hours; by the end of the evening, it would usually be just be Will and me.

At this point, Daryl was getting up at five to go to work, so I started asking him to drop me off at the office on his way. I'd show up at six, so I could hang out with Will for three hours before everyone else came in. This was going on for about two weeks, when Daryl started asking me why I was going into the office so early. Nothing had happened between Will and me yet; I didn't even know for sure how Will felt about me. I mean, okay, it was pretty obvious he liked me, but we didn't discuss anything like that, and he could have had a girlfriend back in New York for all I knew (though I can't imagine when he'd find the time). I did know that I couldn't be dishonest with either Daryl or myself, though, so I did something that I'm still not sure was right. I told Daryl that I was very attracted to someone at work. I told him nothing had happened yet, and I didn't know what or when anything would, but that was enough. Daryl was devastated. He was hurt, and angry, and I lost his trust. At the time I thought being honest was the best thing for both of us, but in retrospect, I know I did it for myself, and I wasn't considering Daryl's feelings at all.

Which is probably why what happened next happened the way it did. Although Will and I were spending as much time together as possible, and there was certainly some flirting involved, we'd never so much as kissed or held hands. Then, one night, after everyone else had left us at the bar, Will and I went back to Thomson, and I found out definitively how Will felt about me. On the floor of my boss's office.

I can't remember if I went home that night. I think I might have, but if I did, I slept alone, because I couldn't share a bed with Daryl after that. I'd agonized over ending my marriage, but for me there wasn't any question anymore. The next day, Will and I went out after work to the usual spot. I remember that we were holding hands, and we'd each had a few drinks, when suddenly Daryl was looming over us, fuming. Will looked at me and asked "Who is this?"

Will knew I was married, but I think we had both consciously chosen not to deal with that aspect of what we were doing. Well, now we were dealing with it. I can't say for sure what happened next, I've probably blocked it out, but I remember being scared, and I'm sure it was not a pretty scene. Even though neither Will nor Daryl is the type to turn a confrontation physical, I just wasn't sure what was going to happen. Daryl had "caught" us, and he was livid, and he was not being quiet about what he thought of me. Probably everyone was staring at us, and I think I was crying.

But, eventually he left, and everything had changed. My marriage really was over, and I couldn't go home.

Will and I went to the Westin Hotel in Copley Plaza that night. Even if he was content sleeping under his desk in the office, I didn't have to tell him that I wouldn't be. (Will had just gotten a check from Thomson, so he paid in cash. He had no credit, I found out later; he said that he'd left a new car on the side of the road when it broke down, and just walked away. He defaulted on the loan and destroyed his credit for seven years.)

I called Daryl the next day, and arranged to come home to get some clothes. Eventually, Daryl would move back to Florida, but for then I told him he could keep the condo, and took up my life at the Westin with Will.

I should have felt bad, and I did, I felt guilty about Daryl, but honestly, I was suddenly having the best time of my life. I'd never felt like this before. We just couldn't get enough of each other. The passion I felt for Will—I realized that this is what people talked about.

I'd only been with three men in my life, and I'd never experienced anything like it. To be completely honest, I'd never even really enjoyed kissing a guy until Will—and sex, well, I thought that was all you get, and if it was no big deal, that was my problem. With Will, I discovered a whole new level of feeling, and realized that this is what it was like to be in love.

So, our lives were pretty good. We'd go to work, we'd go out for lobster dinners at Turner Fisheries or some other wonderful restaurant, we'd send out for room service, and we had each other.

The more I got to know Will, the more I realized he was unlike anyone I'd ever known. He'd do anything, and he always had to do it bigger than anyone else. Even when he had no income, he'd go right ahead anyway. One night, Will found out that I'd never had Indian food, so he took me straight to an Indian restaurant on Newbury Street and ordered practically everything on the menu, so I could sample it all. The waiters were insisting, "Too much food!" but Will was just like that.

Later, when things were tight at Tradeware, when I'd complain to Will that I hated being poor, he'd tell me, "Kerry, we're not poor. We're broke. There's a difference." He was right. It was the difference between living life afraid of what would happen next and living life looking forward to what would happen next, and I'd never lived like this before. It was like a movie, or a good, trashy, romance novel.

***

Daryl and I eventually reached a financial settlement, he left for Florida, and Will and I moved into the condo in Quincy. That's when it really started getting fun.

One day at work, Will went into my boss's office for a meeting, and came out giggling. "Come here, Kerry," he says, and leads me into the stairwell, so he could light a cigarette. "You're not going to believe what I just did."

Even before we got together, Will had been after me to come work for him. "You can't afford me," was what I'd tell him, and the better I got to know him and his circumstances, the less wise a prospect it seemed.

Now, I had left my husband for a guy sleeping under a desk; I wasn't about to quit my job and throw in with a guy who had no regular income.

"I just got a one-year contract, guaranteed, for maintenance on the API."

"How much?" I asked him.

"Eighty grand," he said, and giggled again. That just happened to me my salary at Thomson. Without really knowing it, Thomson was the initial financer of Tradeware, because the next day I gave notice.

Chapter Two

Martin and Rama

While we were still living at the Westin, not long after we got together, Will said, "Let's go up to Maine this weekend, so you can meet my parents. My dad's got a farm up there, with my step-mom Linda."

So we rented a car and drove up. It was a four-hour drive from Boston to Starks, Maine, and we had a blast, talking and laughing all the way. We played childhood car games, and we even played Rock, Paper, Scissors, Will using his right hand to play while he steered with his left. After we'd played a few rounds, Will introduced a typical Will-like wrinkle.

"Rock, paper, scissors, match," we said, and threw our hands in. I went for rock, but when I looked at Will's hand, I didn't recognize his move. He had his thumb stuck up, like a hitchhiker.

"What's that?" I asked. "There's no thumb."

"Dynamite," Will said. "It blows up your rock."

"There's no dynamite in this game! You can't make up a new thing!"

Well, before we'd gone another twenty miles, Will had not only convinced me that I should let him play "dynamite," and that he'd won that round, both of us laughing the whole time, he'd convinced me that adding dynamite made it a much better game. That's how I'm going to teach Trinity to play.

Starks is in the Belgrade Lakes region of Maine, far away from anything, and it was just after Thanksgiving, snowing the whole time. I couldn't believe how much snow there was, and how little of anything else--just trees and snow and little roads that could disappear under the snow at any minute. I'd never been up to Maine before that; I'd never been anywhere that remote, and while I'm basically a city girl, there's a special kind of beauty to it that even I appreciated.

Will found the place, but it wasn't easy. It's up a little dirt road, five miles from the nearest neighbor. We made a wrong turn and got lost in the dark, and ended up on a dairy farm; sitting in the car in the dark, trying to figure out what we had done wrong, we slowly realized we were in the middle of a herd of cows. We figured it all out, though, and eventually, we pulled up to the right place. The only light you could see in all that dark night was coming from the open door of the house, where Ralph and Linda were waiting for us.

I'm not normally a shy person, but I wasn't just meeting new people, these were Will's parents, so I was very subdued when Will said, "Kerry, this is my dad and Linda." I let them do most of the talking.

Linda puts on a tough front, but Ralph is very easygoing, and it all seemed pretty normal. You never would have guessed from how they greeted us—I certainly didn't; I had no idea until Will told me, later, on the way home—that they had not seen Will in nine years, hadn't even known if he was dead or alive until he'd called them the day before, and said, "I met a girl. I'm coming to Maine."

***

Ralph and Linda had last seen Will in 1984, when he was 16. Will had been staying with the two of them in Boston, finishing high school, when he went to a lecture by Dr. Frederick Lenz III. Not long after that, he disappeared.

If that name sounds familiar, and it probably does, chances are that you've heard of him as the author of two best-selling books, *Surfing the Himalayas* and *Snowboarding to Nirvana*. You might have heard of him under his other name, too; Zen Master Rama, the "Yuppie Guru." Rama and his "computer cult" were the subject of a lot of newspaper and magazine articles for a while.

A lot of what Will did with Rama still isn't clear to me. He told me not long after we started talking that he was part of a Buddhist study group, and he later explained that Rama was his mentor, but it was a part of his life he didn't really share with me. He didn't keep it a secret, but it was understood that when he put on his tuxedo to go to a meeting with Rama—and even when he was living under a desk, he had a tuxedo for when Rama called his disciples together—it didn't involve me. Most of what I know about Rama, I've learned on my own, since Will died.

I don't want to betray Will's experience. It was his choice to follow Rama, and he did, till the very end, when Lenz died in 1998, and I know that he learned a lot from him. I learned a lot from Will, so, in a sense,

Rama was my teacher, too. But most of what I've found out about him isn't positive.

In the seventies, Lenz was going to college, working on a degree in English literature, when he became a follower of Sri Chinmoy, a well-known Hindu guru who ran an ashram in Queens, New York. Lenz become one of the best speakers and recruiters for the group, and taught classes at the ashram. He also slept with a lot of the female students, according to people who were there; it seems like that was the main reason that Sri Chinmoy sent him away to San Diego, with instructions to start a West Coast center.

Sometime around then, Lenz started using the name Atmananda. It's pretty obvious from everything he did that he was extremely charismatic and persuasive, like most cult leaders. In San Diego, thousands of people attended his free lectures. Atmananda's followers would then invite specific people from those crowds to study with him for a fee. Sometime around 1980, Lenz announced to his students that negative forces and evil entities had gotten to Sri Chinmoy. Their teacher's teacher, Sri Chinmoy was no longer among the enlightened.

Fortunately, Lenz was now able to reveal that he was among the twelve enlightened beings on earth. (Later, he announced that his favorite dog, Vayu, one of his two black Scotties, was one of the other twelve. Because of Vayu, a lot of his followers had black Scotties, and I can still walk around downtown New York and spot them, walking their black Scotties, always in pairs, like Rama's.) This was not Rama's first incarnation, either. Before he became Frederick Lenz, he had been a holy man in feudal Japan, and a spiritual teacher on Atlantis.

Although Lenz named his post-Sri Chinmoy group Lakshmi, after a Hindu god, he was no longer teaching his followers Hinduism. What he taught now, in lectures, in private sessions, and on the tapes he sold, was composed of bits and pieces of the whole New Age culture that had been gaining ground throughout the seventies: a mix of Hinduism, Zen Buddhism, EST, and Carlos Castaneda, whose Journey to Ixtlan was a favorite book of both Lenz and Will. (Castaneda was a huge influence on the entire alternative spiritual movement, and at this point, pretty commonplace; if a counterculture can be said to have a mainstream, Castaneda is mainstream alternative.) The fees he was charging were changing, too. At first students paid only a few dollars a month, but by the end of the eighties some of his followers were paying him $4000 a month to study with him.

In the early eighties, two things happened that brought Lenz into Will's life (and, in some way, ultimately led Will into my life). Lenz, who had had dropped the name Atmananda and started calling himself Zen Master Rama, decided to move back East, and open a center in Boston. The center never took off, but Lenz spent a lot of money advertising his lectures and classes, in Boston and New York, and he did a lot of recruiting up through the mid-eighties, a lot of it among college students. This is when a lot of people first started to be aware of him. He had big ads in The New York Times and Vanity Fair, and he had billboards up in Times Square. This is also when Will met him.

The other thing that happened was that Lenz, who even his detractors agree was a smart guy, saw that computer programming was going to be a very big thing, and programmers were going to make a lot of money. From the early eighties on, anyone who became part of Lenz's core group of followers was encouraged to quit whatever they were doing—and these were usually bright young people with good careers ahead of them—and study computer programming. It was presented as a discipline that would help to center them and lead them to enlightenment, but once they had the basics down, they were sent out to get consulting jobs and start generating income for Rama. At Lenz's suggestion, they vouched for each other when applying for jobs, using fake names and setting up companies just to supply each other's references.

This is obviously how Will got his start as a programmer, and I know that by the time I left Thompson, a year or two after Will had first started consulting for them, there were probably half a dozen people employed who were part of Rama's group. I have to assume that Will was instrumental in getting them hired, or at least recommended them. Despite what happened later, and the experience other people had, my memory is that they were all excellent programmers. Others, though, were only marginally trained when they started working, and the group as a whole got a bad reputation.

That's when the bad press started. Articles about the computer cult started appearing all over. People found out that one of Rama's followers had committed suicide because he felt he had failed his teacher, and another one overdosed shortly after giving Rama $100,000. Also in the articles were stories about Rama inviting female students to his house for private classes, and then telling them that the fast lane to enlightenment was to have sex with him; sharing his energy would bring them to a higher plane. Some of these women said that they were drugged or threatened with guns if they didn't comply. While all this was going on, Lenz was living the high life, with multiple houses and his own jet. Ultimately, Lenz made many millions of dollars from companies started by his followers; besides the dues he was paid, he was usually given 50% of new companies, and even the patents students filed had his name on them.

But it was also a paranoid life. Lenz was hard to find, not just by the press, when they started looking, but by his followers. Unlike most cult leaders, Rama didn't live with his followers; he was secretive about his whereabouts, moving from house to house, and very guarded about his contacts. It was a way of living that he passed on to his students.

I mentioned before that Will was hard to find, that when I picked up the phone, somebody usually said, "Where's Will?" Partly it was Will's nature, but partly, it was because Rama told his followers that they should be hard to find. Family, friends, even other students, could too easily steal their energies, and pull them backwards on the path to enlightenment. They shouldn't have permanent addresses, he told them, they should always have an answering machine take that their calls, and they should move around a lot.

I know that when Will was in California, he was sharing a house with some other Rama people, and I think that he was at the University of Colorado under Rama's directions, too, possibly recruiting. The trips to

Bora-Bora, to Saba, to the Mauna Lani Bay in Hawaii — all trips he took with other cult members, at Rama's direction. Another thing Rama told his people was that they should cut themselves off from their families, and that's what Will had done, until the day we drove up to Maine to meet his parents.

***

The house in Maine wasn't made for guests; there was a big warm kitchen, and a loft above, where Ralph and Linda slept, so after dinner, when it was time to go to bed, I wondered where we were going to sleep. There was about four feet of snow on the ground when they showed us a futon on the floor of the porch. The porch was glassed in, but it was still the coldest place I've ever slept.

Ralph and Linda went upstairs and Will and I got into bed with all our clothes on and shivered through the night under greatest possible number of blankets. If I'd known that this was Will's homecoming, I might have wondered if this was their cold welcome, but at six or seven in the morning — we were so cold that we didn't get any sleep at all — Will pointed to something and said, "What's that?"

It was an electric heater, which we'd shivered next to for eight hours. Ralph and Linda were not trying to kill us. In fact, now once he'd reconnected with his father, Will and Ralph would become very close; they had a beautiful relationship, and both Ralph and Linda became a big part of our lives. Looking back, despite shivering through the night in subzero weather, and any awkwardness I might have experienced, now that I know the circumstances, I have to say that it was a pretty good visit.

It was also a real eye-opener for me, because I started to learn about Will's past, before Rama.

For one thing, his name wasn't Will—or at least it hadn't been. That first time we visited, Ralph and Linda kept talking about Martin—Martin did this, Martin said that—and I'd be standing there thinking, Who the hell is Martin? Finally, I asked Will and he said, "I'm Martin." Martin is his middle name, and for some family reason—his sister, Karen Michel, has been Michel all her life—that's what people called him, until he disappeared. It took his family years to get used to it, but eventually they all came around to calling him Will, except for Linda, who still sometimes refers to him Martin.

Also, there was going to be a lot more family to meet.

Linda was Ralph's third wife. Will's mother, Ralph's first wife, was Phyllis, who was also the mother of Michel; she remarried a Union Carbide executive who was in charge at the time of the Bhopal disaster, and now she lives in Seattle. Before Will went to Boston to live with Ralph and Linda, though, he'd been living in New Jersey with Karen, Ralph's second wife, along with his half-brother Bill (full name, William Ralph Smithers), and his half-sister Heather.

When Will was a teenager, Ralph still officially lived with Karen and his family in New Jersey, and commuted to Boston for work, but the apartment he kept there for logistical reasons eventually became the place he lived; at some point, Linda started living with him, while he was still married to Karen. When Will went to stay with him there, he wasn't expecting to find his father living with somebody who wasn't his mother or his stepmother, and I'm just guessing, but it might have been an uncomfortable situation for him. On the other hand, I know that he wasn't comfortable in New Jersey, because he told me. He was an outsider, really, who'd come to live with his father, but ended up living with his father's other family — Karen, Bill and Heather — while his father lived in Boston, and he never really felt like be belonged there.

Will's half-brother Bill was to become a big part of Will's life after they were back in touch, and we both came to love him. Ralph had called Bill up immediately after hearing from Will, and when Bill was back on the East Coast for Christmas just a few weeks later, he came to see Will.

Bill had always held onto a lot of good memories of Will living with his family in New Jersey, but they were the worshipful memories of a little kid for a teenager; a six-year difference might not seem like much to adults in their twenties and thirties, but back then, it was too big a gap for Bill to provide Will with the sort of companionship that might have made him feel welcome and at home.

That first visit in Quincy, though, Bill and Will never stopped talking, as if they'd been in the middle of a conversation that had been put on hold, and now they could pick up right where they left off, except as adults and equals. Actually, they must have stopped talking sometime, to drink, anyway, because they were both pretty drunk by the end of the night. I also have a blurry memory (it wasn't like I abstained; I wasn't the designated memoirist yet) of Bill fully clothed, asleep in the bathtub.

Bill's memories of Will as a teenager are of a super-bright and very science-minded kid, always coming up with interesting projects, like the Fourth of July Will announced, "Screw fireworks. I'm making bombs," and built bombs in Twinnings tea cans, and then blew them up all over the property; or the Christmas he set up a still in the basement and everybody in the family got little bottles of something Will called Smithers XXX as gifts. (The consensus is that it was awful stuff.)

Will brought that same rational, scientific, turn of mind to his first meeting with Rama, too. One night, after they'd reconnected, and had starting going camping together, while sitting around a campfire in Chalice, Idaho, Will told Bill that he went to that first Rama lecture as a skeptic, just waiting to take apart all the crap that the gullible suckers were falling for, but the power of Rama made him let go of his skepticism.

As far as I can tell, he never again looked at Rama through that kind of strictly rational lens. After nine years of separation from his family, though, he must have put aside at least part of what Rama said, because he was no longer in hiding.

Chapter Three

Sandblasting, Motorcycles, and How to Get Paid

By May of 1993, Tradeware was up and running. We rented an office at 355 Congress Street, across the street from Thomson, and opened up for business. It was just me and Will. We quickly got two clients in addition to Thomson: Merrill Lynch, and Robinson Humphrey, an investment bank in Atlanta. It was a pretty shabby office. For furniture, all we had were some tables from Staples and a water cooler—we were so proud of our water cooler. There was a Sparc 1 server, and Will's little laptop—I still have it; it's under my desk, broken now, and, of course, obsolete by a number of generations. The office was a little embarrassing, so whenever we had client meetings Will would take them across the street and use a conference room at Thomson. Since he was in and out of there all the time, servicing their contract, everybody at Thomson assumed he was supposed to be there, so nobody ever noticed.

Not long after we moved, a couple of months or so, we decided it was time to make our office more presentable. We weren't going to get away with borrowing a conference room forever. Instead of just painting, or hiring somebody to do the work for us, though, our delusions of grandeur led us to decide to sandblast the walls — and to do it ourselves. That was Will, really, but I went along, and here is the lesson we learned from that experience: sandblasting is something you never want to do yourself.

Will got one of his friends to come in and help, another cult guy, actually, and we covered everything with plastic sheets, or thought we did, anyway, and then I went out and took a walk. I remember walking back at the end of the day, coming down the street and looking up and just stopping. There were huge clouds of dust billowing from the windows, and the generator was so loud you couldn't hear anything else — which is fortunate, because it was probably setting off car alarms. I made my way to the building and up the stairs through thick clouds of dust, and when I walked in, the office looked like the surface of the moon. Everything was covered with inches of fine dust.

To this day, anything that we kept from that office still has dust in it.

Because this was an old building, it wasn't just our office, though. The building was "leaky," and dust went everywhere. We sandblasted over the weekend, and got a start on cleaning up our office, but it wasn't until Monday morning that we found out how bad it really was. It went upstairs, it went downstairs; the dust got into the offices all around us, and all the other tenants in the building were absolutely pissed off at us. We got into a court fight over it, because there was a photographer on the floor above us who said a lot of his stuff had been destroyed.

Then we had to get rid of all the dust and debris. We hadn't realized it was hazardous waste, and there were bags full of it. It took us all week to find somewhere to dump it, and when we did, Will insisted that we do it at night, to maintain plausible deniability, one of his favorite expressions. But no matter what we did or how much we cleaned, there was still dust everywhere, and finally, because of that, and the tenant upstairs—the headquarters for a chain of hairdressers, where it seemed like everybody wore high heels and didn't have desks, because they spent the day walking back and forth on the hardwood floors, driving us crazy—we decided to just move Tradeware back to Quincy. We still had most of the year on the lease, and we weren't going to get out of it, so we lost some money, but we hard-forwarded the phones and for the rest of the time we were Boston, we worked out of my condo.

Before we moved out, though, one of the tenants we were still friendly with, a small courier with an office downstairs, stopped me in the lobby.

"Hey," he told me, full of enthusiasm, "I'm going to sandblast, too."

I just looked at him. I thought he must be joking, but he wasn't. After I told Will, we stopped by his office just to say, "Are you sure this is something you want to do?" but he was determined. Unfortunately, while we knew enough to try to talk him out of it, we hadn't thought it through. We didn't cover the equipment in our office up the weekend he said he was going to sandblast, and lost a computer to more dust

***

For somebody as brilliant at coding as Will was, he sure hated coding. The day I started coding for Tradeware, he stopped, and he just about never wrote another line of code for Tradeware. (He did, however, enthusiastically code away all night when it was for one of his hobbies, like diving.) Will was the salesman, running back and forth from New York City, making sales calls. So, usually with my cats, Zach and Asia, as my only company, I stayed in the apartment and wrote code, sometimes for 12 or 14 hours a day. It was the first time I ever worked from home. One of the problems of working out of the apartment was that Zach, who had a very loud voice, would start talking to Will and I whenever we were on the phone. If it was a client, we'd have to rush to get Zach out of the room before the client heard his loud, demanding, and very unprofessional meows.

Will took to my cats right away when he moved in with me, and he always particularly liked Zach. We called Zach the "periphery cat," because he always maintained his catlike diffidence, never wanting to jump on your lap, or get right in the middle of the action; he preferred to hang out and relax somewhere nearby where he could keep an eye on things without actually participating, usually in your peripheral vision. Will said he was like the lovable, shabby, uncle who dozed in the recliner.

Will was constantly trying to get me sell him Zach. He liked Zach so much that he wanted him to officially be "his" cat. It was half a joke, and he'd have me laughing about it, but he was also serious. He really wanted

Zach, and he'd bring it up all the time, raising the offer, but I consistently and flatly refused. Zach was not for sale.

Zach was the Z in Zplan, the dive planning software that Will wrote, which was widely adopted in the technical diving community. If you visit the zplan website, zplan.com, you'll find a nice picture of the late, famous, Zacharia Moose Cat.

Also, when you don't have an office to go to, things can just get weird, unless you establish your own routine. Will would be gone, and I'd be immersed in coding, and suddenly I would sit up and realize it had been a week since I'd left the apartment. So I started running. Will got me started; he didn't keep it up, because his knees couldn't take it, but he got me out there, and I was eventually doing two miles a day. I was in the best shape of my life. I'd get up, go for a run, two miles along Marina Bay, and then come home and code all day, and that was my life. Neither of us cooked, so we sent out for pizza a lot.

Eventually, it occurred to me that if I was going to work my butt off, I wanted a stake in the company. Will had drawn up the papers for Tradeware before I left Thomson, so when I joined him, I was an employee, not a partner. I told Will, "Hey, it's just you and me here. I want half."

"Well, I can't give you half," Will told me.

"Why not?"

That's when I found out that Rama owned 50 percent of the company. Will had probably started the company because Rama said he should, and when he drew up the papers, Rama was an equal partner.

There was nothing I could do about that, but I still wanted equity. I ended up hiring a lawyer, and I fought for my piece of the company. I ended up with seven percent. It came out of Will's fifty percent, of course, so Rama owned the largest piece of the company. Rama was our silent partner.

I realized that was a problem not long after I became the third partner in Tradeware.

We always had some income, because we never borrowed money from anybody; we always had enough to get through. But there was a point when we'd run through the eighty thousand from Thomson, and things were pretty tight. We'd just gotten a small check, for about five thousand dollars, from Merrill Lynch. The first thing Will did was make out a check to Rama for twenty-five hundred dollars, fifty percent off the top, which at that moment in Tradeware's financial history was basically half of the company's liquid assets.

I didn't know anything at all about Rama then, other than what Will told me. He was Will's adviser, and Will was certain that he was instrumental to whatever success he'd had so far. I didn't know exactly why Rama owned half of the company, but really, I trusted Will, and if he had decided to do that, I was sure he had a good reason.

When Will made out that check, though, I had to put my foot down. This was something I couldn't tolerate. It wasn't the first check to Rama; Will had been doing this from the start, and I knew it, but things hadn't been so tight, and also, it wasn't my money then. So I said, "Will, you can't run a business this way. This is crazy. You can't do fifty percent off the top. If you don't do something about this, there's no way we're ever going to get out of this apartment. We're never going to have an office. We're never going to have a staff. We're never going to be anything. You've got to talk to him."

Will always used to laugh at me and say, "Kerry, your whole emotional well-being is based on the balance in your checkbook." He said it then.

I said "Yeah? Fine. I can live with that. I can't live with fifty percent off the top. Now go talk to Rama."

And he did. He had a meeting with Rama, and Rama told him that he didn't have to pay his "dues." So that was the end of that. Or so we thought at the time, anyway.

It's hard enough to get a new company going under normal conditions, so it's incredible that we made it through at all; until I made my stand, Will was turning over half of every dollar we made to Rama. We were flying on one wing the whole time, but we never went down.

It got close, though.

There was a time when we were counting on a check from Robinson Humphries in Atlanta. We'd been working for them for months and our phone bill by itself was $8,000 a month, because I was dialing into their server in Atlanta for eight hours a day to test everything. They owed close to $60,000, but they had a bad case of what we call just-one-more-itis. You say "Pay me" and they say, "Yes, we're sending your money, but first you have to do this, and this, and this." Then, once you get those fixes done, it's one more thing, and you never get paid. That's how a lot of software companies get into trouble, because they keep doing that to you.

We were running out of money pretty fast, and that's what Robinson Humphries was doing to us. So, finally, I said, "Forget this." I told Will, "Okay. I'm done waiting," and I put a time bomb in their next software update. I set it up so that as of a specific date, the software wouldn't work anymore. I left a little variable that would let me override the trigger remotely, of course.

Now, this wasn't software that we were still testing; they were running their trading floor with it. However long it was went by, and they still didn't pay. I'd written a printout into the application that would say *License expires in ten days*, and I expected to hear from them, but obviously nobody was checking the logs that got printed out by their server to record the day's processes.

As the deadline approached, I told Will, "Their trading floor is going to stop working in ten days." He wanted to wait and see if anyone noticed, but when there were only three days left until the whole operation shut down, we decided to call and tell them. Will had a pretty good relationship with the head trader there, Sandy Purdy. Sandy would call here and say, "Tell Will his mentor is on the phone." (He was joking, mostly because he was older than Will, but also because people didn't really talk about having "mentors," in the early nineties. Of course, Sandy had no way of knowing that the job was already taken; not only did Will already have a mentor, the mentor owned half the company Sandy was doing business with.)

So, Will called and said, "Sandy, I don't want to be pushy, but you owe me some money."

"Well, um, yes, of course...we'll be getting that to you."

"No, Sandy. We've been talking about this money for a long time and I have to tell you, your software's about to stop working."

"*What?*"

"Yeah, I'm afraid it's all shutting down if we don't get paid."

"When?"

"In three days."

He could tell we weren't bluffing. We had a check for $60,000 the next day. I thought they might be mad, but they were the ones playing games and we all knew it.

That incident in 1994 with Robinson Humphries evolved into the licensing scheme I use today. Over the course of time, we instituted the concept of quarterly licensing, and I made it all smarter. Now we have an automatic license generator and they're all encrypted licenses. It's been one of the keys to Tradeware's success—you don't pay, the software stops working. It's a pretty effective approach.

***

Tradeware wasn't out of the woods yet, though, in part because we were determined not to borrow. So, when we came to another serious money crunch, we didn't consider going to a bank, or looking for venture capital, or asking my family for a loan. Instead, I started eyeing Will's Harley.

The green Fat Boy was Will's second bike. One of the things that happened after Will and I went up to Maine to see Ralph and Linda was that Will almost immediately bought a motorcycle, a Harley Soft Tail. Motorcycles are one of Ralph's real enthusiasms; Ralph and Bill, Will's half-brother, took camping trips out West together as often as they could. As soon as Will heard this, he told them to count him in. Will went back up to Maine, he and Ralph went shopping, and when Will came back to Quincy, he was riding on a Harley.

He started riding back and forth from Boston to Maine to visit, and they started planning to go on a real trip. Will didn't like the Soft Tail because of the vibration, though, and I agreed wholeheartedly. It was on that bike that I took my first and only motorcycle trip with Will. We rode up to Maine, me sitting behind Will, wishing I were somewhere else. Anywhere else. It was horrible. I discovered I really didn't like motorcycle rides.

I didn't think it could get worse, but when we were supposed to leave, we woke up in the morning, and it was pouring. I didn't want to go, but Ralph and Linda took me out to the barn, and pulled out all this rain gear and put me on the back of the motorcycle. I was terrified, the whole three-hour trip back to Quincy in the rain, and I was crying for most of it. Riding on the back of a motorcycle in the pouring rain for three hours is no fun.

Linda suggested that if I got my own bike, I'd have a lot more fun, but I decided that was something I didn't need to explore. I never got on a motorcycle again.

Will, though, went through four, in just a few years. Ralph directed him to the Fat Boy, with a rubber-mounted engine for a smoother ride, and Will traded up. But before Will got to ride it out West, we ran into that financial rough spot I mentioned, and it felt like the only option we had was selling the Harley. Will agreed, and the next weekend, Will got on his bike, and I got in the car behind him, and we drove up to this place in

Nashua, New Hampshire that Ralph had told us about. There was an auction there every Saturday, a place people go when they want to turn a bike into cash fast, and that's what we did. The Fat Boy went up on the block, and the next thing you know, Will's holding $15,000 in cash.

We looked at each other with huge grins, because it was such a relief to know that Tradeware was going to stay in business for a while longer (and of course because we were going to continue eating). Will laid out all the money on the dashboard, just to look at it on the way home. Yes, I was afraid it would all go flying out the window, but fortunately, it didn't.

***

Will did finally join Bill and Ralph on their camping trips, later, after we moved to New York. Ralph was then spending a lot of time out in Salt Lake City where Bill lived, because they were starting up a restaurant together, The Sugarhouse Barbecue Company. Will, Ralph, Linda and Bill were equal partners in the place.

With Ralph and Bill out there, Will flew out and bought a BMW motorcycle (after a trip on Harleys plagued by mechanical problems, they all switched overnight and became BMW enthusiasts), which he kept out there, in Bill's or Ralph's garage. Will never had a bike in New York.

Their first trip was just a long weekend in Southern Utah, out in the desert. Bill's girlfriend drove a pickup truck with all the camping gear, so it was an easy trip. After that, though, they took a trip up into Canada; through British Columbia up to Alaska (through a town called Smithers, where they stopped to pose with the sign), across to the Queen Charlotte Islands and down through Vancouver Island and Victoria. It was on that trip that Will decided to become a gourmet cook.

They'd been traveling all week, deciding each day what they were going to eat, and then stopping at a market for supplies. One day, Ralph and Bill decided that they were going to make coq au vin. Will didn't believe them. He figured there was no way they could do that with nothing but the equipment they carried for camping. But they got everything they needed, and Ralph and Bill proceeded to make a wonderful coq au vin.

Will was always incredibly funny, and when he said to them, "This is awesome. And if idiots like you two can cook this out here in the middle of nowhere, I can become a gourmet cook," they laughed, but he was serious. He did it, and that became another thing Will shared with Ralph. After he got home from that trip, Will was on the phone with Ralph every day, trading cooking tips, sharing recipes, telling him the latest variation in a sauce he'd made.

Just like everything else, when Will did something, he had to do it better than anyone would have thought possible. It wasn't long before I started looking forward to the elaborate dinners Will was cooking up. It sure beat the pizzas we sent out for when we were living in the apartment in Quincy.

Chapter 4

Operation Boxfish

In Quincy, I kept a humidifier running all the time, because the air in the condo was so dry. When my cat, Zach, wasn't meowing his objections to me paying attention to clients on the phone instead of him, he used to sit and watch the humidifier, waiting for one of those bubbles that "bloop" up every once in a while.

One day, Will said "Zach really loves that humidifier, doesn't he?"

"Yeah. Isn't it funny?"

"I bet he'd really love a fish tank."

I'd never considered getting pets for my cat before, but Will was enthusiastic, and I was game. We found a fish store in Boston, and once he saw the more expensive, elaborate setups, of course,

Will was never going to be satisfied with a little tank and some goldfish. Will decided we needed a marine tank full of the prettiest, most exotic, fish.

Marine tanks are delicate saltwater environments, and difficult to maintain. Will was immediately engaged. I can tell you now that a saltwater aquarium is all about nitrates and oxygenation, and the reason that I know that is just from being around Will. Whatever Will became interested in, he always took to a Ph. D. level. Just from watching him and listening to him, I learned more about aquariums (and eventually, diving, but I'll get to that later) than most of the people you'll find selling them in pet stores.

We brought home a 45-gallon tank and a couple of fish, and Will starting cycling the water, trying to get just the right chemical balance in the tank. My grandfather always used to say, "Kids are like pancakes. You always throw out the first batch"—which, being the oldest, I didn't really appreciate—and unfortunately, it's true for fish in saltwater tanks, too. You have to be ready to sacrifice the first fish in your tank while you get everything adjusted.

After two weeks, Will got the tank stabilized, and we went out and bought our second "batch" of fish, the ones you keep: a bright, spotted boxfish, a porcupine fish, the spiky kind that puffs up into a ball, and some tangs, which flash bright colors when their iridescent scales catch the light. Will was right. Zach loved it. He'd sit for hours watching the fish. The humidifier was forgotten, the Betamax of Zach-entertainment-formats.

Will was content for about a minute. "That's cool," he said, when it was all done and Zach was planted in front of that first aquarium. But then he really started getting into it. He started experimenting with all sorts of corals, brain corals and bubble corals; all sorts of things. Then he realized what we really needed were expensive halogen lights, and once he had that taken care of, it became obvious to him that what he *really* needed was a bigger tank, and that was just the start.

So, what began as home entertainment for my cat turned into a multi-thousand dollar pursuit that led to the huge, gorgeous, 45-gallon reef tanks in our first office in New York at 99 Wall Street. We had a pretty elaborate setup in Quincy, and transporting to New York and getting them in tanks in time to keep them alive wasn't going to be easy, but in the summer of 1995, we decided it was time for Tradeware to move to Wall Street.

Will had been traveling back and forth to New York from the time we started up Tradeware, while I stayed home and coded. Before 1995 we didn't have a laptop fast enough for Will to do demos on, which meant he had to lug computer components with him all over the place. He was traveling with a Sun workstation the size of a giant pizza box, and monitors back then were still enormous. It all went on a cart, and it was a major pain. Almost all our clients were in New York by then, and even more important, that's where all our potential business was; all of Will's sales calls were on Wall Street. So, finally, Will came back from New York one day and said, "Screw this. This sucks. We're moving to New York."

I had only been to New York City once. The Securities Industries Association had their big annual trade show in New York, and I'd gone with Will the year before.

Until then, our business had been all back-office stuff. We were providing servers the brokers used to process their trades, and once they were set up, only IT people really interacted with them, or I'd dial in from Boston and take care of things from home.

That year, though, Robinson Humphries, our client in Atlanta, had started saying, "Well, this is great, but we want to be able to manipulate those trades as they're going through our system." This was a whole new thing for us. If they wanted brokers and salespeople to get involved in the process, we had to start thinking about building front ends. They were going to need a desktop application with a graphical user interface that brought it all together for the end users, designed so they wouldn't have to get their hands dirty and they couldn't break anything.

This turned out to be one of the few occasions when Will returned to writing code for Tradeware. He obsessed for three days, doing nothing but work on this app. If we were going to build front ends, he told me, they were going to look really really cool. He created a console with a metallic, three-dimensional appearance, which was great, but the real touch of genius was that he thought to put screws in the four corners, which was not just cool, but really funny. "Eye-candy," he called it. It was just like Will. You had to stop and think, and then you had to laugh.

That became MarketCenter, and Will was right. We showed it at the SIA that year and people loved it. Everyone thought it looked great, and from then on people would ask us, "Are you the ones with the screws?" We were known as the "screw people" (which could be good or bad, depending on the context, but we certainly made an impression). People in the industry kept asking what tool kit we used to build it, but it was all proprietary, cooked from scratch. Today, the screws Will drew are in the front ends of all our desktop products.

So that was Tradeware's debut. We went to SIA as a firm for the first time that summer, with this cool new product, and got a great response. What was funny was that nobody knew was that our booth in the New York Hyatt wasn't just representing our company at the show—it *was* our company. That was everything right there. Will and I were the staff, and we'd brought along all our equipment to do demos.

But that didn't seem to hurt us. Will loved to bluff, and he always got away with it. We even got a deal from that show, with a San Francisco firm called Rosenberg Institutional Equities. After they saw MarketCenter we talked for a while and they put in an order.

There was only one problem. We had just sold vaporware again.

The buzz that year through the whole industry was something called FIX (Financial Information eXchange). The FIX protocol is a set of software specifications designed to facilitate communications in the financial industries. It had been hammered out between Fidelity Investments and Salomon Brothers as a framework for electronic trading, so that the IT people at both firms had a common language. In 1994 they had given out copies of the protocols at the SIA.

That year, Will had come back to Boston from the SIA and handed me the manual. "I have seen the future," he told me, "and it is FIX."

(Will liked to make pronouncements, and they were always funny, because he had such a great sense of humor, and because of the perspective he had on himself. When he made them—like when he'd finish writing some tricky code, and then declare "I am a programming GOD"—he was half serious, but he realized how he sounded, and put a twist on it that let you know he was in on the joke, too. Sometimes, he'd stand in front of the mirror admiring his hair after he'd gotten it cut and announce, "Is this not perfect hair? Kerry, you are in the presence of perfect hair.")

Will was being funny that day when he predicted the future, but that time he was completely serious, too. He was also right. FIX was the thing that really made Tradeware the huge success it became. We were perfectly positioned to become FIX pioneers when Will saw how important FIX could be. As the first suppliers on Wall Street to implement the FIX protocol in their products, we claimed a "first mover" advantage which continues to make us innovators and leaders in the industry.

Unfortunately, Robinson Humphries was firmly situated in the present, so the MarketCenter product we'd put together for them wasn't FIX compliant. After we assured Rosenberg Institutional Equities that it was, I had to run back home and redo the whole thing to FIX specifications.

So, that's how things stood when we decided to move to New York. I put the condo on the market, and Will started looking for an office. Before he moved to Boston, Will had been living in a little studio on Pearl Street, and the apartment had been taken over by his friend Davide (Will knew him from Rama circles; they'd lived together at least once, in California, but they'd both been moving around a lot with the group, and it might have been more than that). That's the place Will told me about when we started to get to know each other, where he'd run an extension cord in from the hall after his electricity got cut off. David was in Korea when we came to New York, so we moved in there for the first few months.

The office was another story. Will got in touch with a realtor, and after he finished his day's business, he'd go with her to see a bunch of offices every day, and call afterward to tell me about each space he saw. Will had some very specific requirements, and it took him a while to find the right place.

First of all, Will insisted we get an office that was actually on Wall Street, which is where our clients were, but it's also where the power was. Will was always very aware of the energies around him, and he wanted our office to be on major power lines, and they had to be the right ones. He explained to me that Wall Street was a tricky place when it came to that sort of thing because there was so much power there, and not all of it was positive.

Ever since I'd met him, Will had talked about energy and power lines and things like that, things that he had learned from Rama. While I never doubted that he was talking about something real, I took it on faith, because it wasn't something I had experienced myself.

Later, after we'd been in New York for a while, we looked at an apartment right across from the New York Stock Exchange. It was gorgeous, and logistically perfect. The apartments were huge and they were already wired for T1. But that was the first time I really got what Will was talking about when he said "bad energy." I was immediately uncomfortable there, and then, walking down the hall, I actually saw the dead twins from *The Shining*. My skin was crawling until we got back out onto the street. When we left, we both said "That was just nasty." I finally really knew what Will had been talking about, and it made sense that the energy would be so strong there.

But while Will was looking for our first office, I trusted his instincts, and he finally found an office for us on the 24th floor of 99 Wall Street. I put my condo on the market and we began the move.

Because Tradeware consisted of Will, me and a couple of computers, and personally neither one of us had accumulated much in the way of "stuff," Will was able to move almost everything to New York in a couple of trips with a rented U-Haul. The hard part was Operation Boxfish: getting our six tropical fish to New York without killing them. It was a pretty complicated undertaking. We didn't actually synchronize our watches, but it felt like we did, and I could almost hear the Mission Impossible music playing in the background the whole time.

In New York, Will bought a new 90-gallon tank and installed it in the office. The morning of the move, he started cycling the water to get it ready. I had gone to Home Depot and bought a big Playmate cooler and a bunch of plastic bins. The live rock—corals and rocks inhabited by worms and little shrimp that are part of the tank's ecosystem—went into the small containers, and I filled the cooler with water from the tank. That's when the race began. I started catching fish and scooping them into the cooler, and then broke down and loaded up the rest of the aquarium.

It took me all day to get everything done. At about 8, I called Will to tell him to be ready. I put the fish in their cooler on the seat beside me, and started down to New York. I was worried about those poor fish being bounced around in the pitch dark of the cooler, so I kept pulling over to the side of the road and McDonald's into parking lots to check and make sure they were okay.

The ride took about four hours, and I got there at midnight. The security guard at 99 Wall Street had never seen me before, and at first didn't know what to make of the frantic woman with the big cooler shouting, "Hurry up! I have fish! I have fish! They have to get to the 24th floor!"

Will was up there waiting, of course, and we transferred them into the new tank immediately—even though they're supposed to get acclimated in an intermediate tank—but we were proud to say that we didn't lose a single fish. All six of them survived the move.

Except for the aquariums—we now had a 45 gallon tank and a 90-gallon tank, and Will would soon start experimenting with incredibly delicate and complicated reef tanks, too—we had almost nothing in the way of furniture. We had a card table from Staples with my computer on it, a couple of chairs, and that was about it. I think there was also a milk crate, for formal staff meetings.

From the start, I was always at my desk—or card table, anyway—first thing in the morning, nine o'clock. That's just my nature. Will ran on a different schedule. He was a night person, and now that we had an office, it became obvious that what he meant by office hours wasn't what everybody else meant by office hours. Even then, when we first set up Tradeware at 99 Wall Street, I'd usually be at work for an hour or two before Will arrived. (It got later and later over the next few years, until Will was arriving at the office just in time to ask if anybody wanted to go get a drink, because everyone would be leaving for the day.)

One morning, within days of the move, I left Will sleeping at Pearl Street, and was coding away at the office when Will came in and said, "Kerry, you're not going to believe what just happened. I was walking here from the apartment, and out on the sidewalk in front of Goldman Sachs is a whole crew of guys loading old office furniture into a truck. I asked the foreman what was going on, and he told me they were hauling it away to be demolished. So I asked if I brought over a U-Haul, would he load the furniture into there instead. He didn't care where he loaded the furniture, his job was just to get rid of it, so I got the U-Haul and they loaded it up. It looks like we missed all the really good stuff, all that was left was pretty beaten up, but I just furnished our office."

"That's great," I said, "but how are we going to get it up here?"

"Don't worry about it. I gave the foreman $500 and told him to meet me here with a couple of guys at five o'clock. I'll bring the U-Haul over, and they'll bring it up."

I couldn't believe Will had already given them the money and really expected them to show up. "They're never going to show," I told him. Will shook his head at my lack of faith, and we argued for the rest of the day about whether the guys were going to show up. They did, of course. Will had gotten desks for both of us, a conference table and a reception desk, and some wooden chairs. It was all in that traditional, heavy, somber, Wall Street style. If it was also very obviously used, we figured that just made us look like we'd been there for a while, which isn't a bad thing.

Now that we had furniture, the office need to be painted, too. Apparently, we hadn't learned our lesson from sandblasting the office in Boston, because we decided that we would do it ourselves, over the Labor Day weekend. We went to Home Depot and equipped ourselves for a painting marathon; Will, with his usual enthusiasm, jumped on the opportunity to get one of those "As Seen On TV" gadgets, a PowerRoller.

He had a great time, but I was just using the usual rollers and brushes, and by two in the morning, I'd had enough. (And a week later, I couldn't figure out where the mysterious pain in my shoulders was from, until I realized it got worse when I reached up above my head—the same motion I made painting the walls.)

I talked Will into quitting for the night, and after we did a little cleanup, we headed out. When the elevator came, the security guard was in it, doing his rounds.

Now, I had gotten stuck in this same elevator a week before, all by myself in this steel box for about half an hour. That time, I hit the alarm, and the building staff came to rescue me. I had to jump through a side door they opened, into the other elevator. It wasn't far, but it was still pretty hairy.

Well, that was scary enough (and it was the beginning of a pretty severe case of claustrophobia that still bothers me), but when we got in the elevator with the security guard a week later and got stuck again, I would have completely lost it, except that Will was with me. With him there, I was able to remain pretty calm. Unfortunately, the guard did not get the same feelings of security from Will's presence that I did, and he immediately began to freak out. In his defense, he was also the first one of us to realize that everybody in the building was right there in that elevator, and nobody was going to come rescue us for at least another two days.

Will, of course, saw the whole thing as an challenge and an adventure, and immediately pulled out his Swiss Army knife. I was stuck in an elevator with McGuyver, which, if you think about it, isn't the worst thing that can happen. He started examining the walls to see how to get us out, which is when he noticed that the fan wasn't working. "It's going to get hot in here pretty soon," he announced.

The guard really started to panic, then, and while Will and I tried to calm him down, he franticly started trying to pry the doors open by himself. Will said, "Save your strength, man. There's no way you're going to get the door open," but I thought I saw the door move a little bit, so we all started pushing, and eventually we got it open.

We had been stuck between the thirteenth and fourteenth floors, so when we finally escaped, we still had to get out of the building. We pressed the button to get the other elevators, but when the first one came and we started to get in, Will shouted, "NO! You in that one, me in this one, you in that one." We each took a separate car, so if one of the elevators got stuck, two of us would make it down and could get help.

We didn't get stuck again. We went back and finished painting over a couple of days, but only because we were extremely lazy about it. We really did no more than a surface job. If there were shelves we didn't move them, and if a desk was up against a wall, we left it there and painted around it.

With the office furnished and painted, I turned my attention to our living situation, because the studio on Pearl Street was so small that even our cats were getting depressed and complaining about it. We only stayed there for a month. I didn't know my way around New York, but I was able to figure out that Battery Park City was just a short walk from Wall Street. That's all it took for me to say, "Okay, we're going to live there."

We took the first apartment we saw, a little one bedroom. We lived in two other apartments there, but we stayed in Battery Park City, in the shadow of the World Trade Center, until after that shadow was gone.

Chapter Five

Islands

One day, while he was tinkering with the aquariums, Will asked me if I'd ever been scuba diving. This was in 1994, before we'd moved to New York, when he was really involved with the complicated aspects of saltwater aquariums, which I guess is what made him think of it. Will had done some diving when he was living in California, but it had never even occurred to me to try it.

"That's it," he said. "We're getting certified. It's lots of fun. You'll have a great time."

"Doesn't it take, like, six or eight weeks to get certified? In classes with a bunch of other people? That's just not us, Will."

"That's how other people get certified," he told me. "Don't worry about it."

Will got on the computer (before Netscape and the web came along, people like Will were communicating on the Internet through a system called Usenet, made up of what now look like primitive mailing groups, but it put you in touch with people and information all over the world) and a day or two later, he came up with the name of a guy in North Salem, not too far away. The guy was a certified PADI (Professional Association of Diving Instructors) instructor, and he was authorized to give us the written part of the test after we put in a certain number of hours practicing in a swimming pool.

This guy worked with his girlfriend, and Will arranged for the two of them to spend a weekend with us doing the pool work, and then on Sunday, he'd give us the tests. Will picked up all the books with all the PADI course material, and diligent little nerd that I am, I spend the week before the test studying. I noticed immediately that Will wasn't.

"You know, Will, if you don't join me and do some studying, you're going to fail the test." I got Will's "Oh ye of little faith" look.

"I don't need to study," Will told me. "I know all of this stuff already."

That's when things got competitive. It was fun, but we were serious. I was as determined to do better on the test as he was, and he was now committed to not cracking a book the whole time, because, you know, Will knows everything.

That weekend came and we drove up to North Salem. We met them at the local YMCA. Will went into the pool with the instructor, and I went in with the girlfriend, and over two days we basically crammed in the entire six week class. When it came time to take the test on Sunday, the instructor, who had been listening to us go back and forth all weekend about who's going to get a higher score, said, "Normally, I'd stick around to make sure you don't cheat and help each other, but that's obviously not going to happen," and he handed us the tests and went across the street to McDonald's.

It was a multiple-choice test, and by the time he came back to check on us, we'd already finished and matched our answers against each other. There were only four questions where we'd chosen different answers.

Will showed him the tests, and said, "You don't have to check our answers; we both got all of them right except for those four. Just tell us which of us got those right."

So the guy, who already knew that we had the material down, got out the answer key and start checking those four questions. The first one, I got right. The second one, Will was right, so we were even. The third one, me again. Then, on the fourth one, which was a tricky question about J-valves and K-valves on tanks, the instructor checked the key, and my answer was right. Will immediately protested. Now, I knew I was right, because the question and answer came right out of the books, and I'd been studying. But Will insisted that the question was ambiguous, and explained how under certain circumstances his answer was right, and in general just refused to give up. By the time he was done, he had argued the instructor into giving both of us credit for the question.

Still, though, I got a 98 and he got a 96. This time, the cocky grasshopper came close, but the nerdy ant won.

With the written test passed, we got referrals for our certification dives. So, right before we moved to New York, we took our first diving trip, to Grand Cayman Island. If you've ever seen the movie *The Firm*, you probably remember the hotel that Tom Cruise stayed in, the Hyatt on Grand Cayman. We stayed in the same place, and it was beautiful.

When we first met, Will had told me about all the trips he'd taken, to places like Mauna Lani and Bora Bora, and we'd talked about how we wanted to do things like that together, and now, a few years later, here we were. From then on, we'd take a trip every six weeks or so. It was our escape; our pressure release valve (although we'd probably argue about whether it was a J-valve or a K-valve) . Whatever was going on with Tradeware, we'd try to find the time to go off to some beachy island for diving.

That was the first time I'd been diving, and I have to admit that I found it a little scary. I have my claustrophobia issues, and diving combines the claustrophobia of being in that little mask and hearing your own breathing with all that water pressing in on you, and the agoraphobia of being in that vast blue space. I kept in control and didn't panic, though. I remembered what everyone said: In diving all you have to do is remember to breathe.

The first day we did two dives, and I did okay, and Will, of course, had no problem. We did our third and fourth dive the next day, and that was it: we were certified. A few weeks later, we'd get our cards in the mail.

After the last dive, we were on the beach, celebrating with a few other people who had also gotten certified. We were all in a good mood and a little drunk, when Will came back with the third or fourth round of drinks, and, without ever having mentioned he was going to, tells me, "Oh, by the way, I signed us up for a night dive."

"Are you out of your mind?" I asked him. I'd managed to make it through four dives without panicking, but now Will had me going down at night for my first post-certification dive, and after drinking all afternoon.

"Oh, c'mon, Kerry. It'll be fun. It's not even really a night dive. It's at dusk, just as the sun's going down.," I was reluctant, but he persuaded me. So, there I was, a couple of hours later, on a boat with a dozen other people getting ready for a night dive, knowing you're never supposed to dive when you've been drinking. I was having second thoughts, or really, I was having first thoughts a second time, since all the reasons not to go were my initial response.

But Will and I got in the water and started down the mooring line. I hadn't gone ten feet when I knew I wasn't going any further. It's one thing to be surrounded by vast blue spaces, but down here, everything was just black. Who knew what was swimming a few feet away, just out of reach of the flashlight? I signaled for Will to surface with me, and when we got back up I told him there was no way I was doing this. I hated to spoil Will's fun, but I just couldn't do it. Fortunately, a couple in our diving party overheard us, and invited Will to be their third buddy, so it all worked out. I spent the rest of the dive on the boat.

To this day, I haven't completed a night dive. I tried again, years later, after I'd gotten much more comfortable being underwater. I went out with a group of about ten people, but before we even got in the water people's regulators were failing, and the current started kicking up, and we ending up calling the dive off because it just wasn't safe. At that point, I concluded I wasn't meant to make a night dive, and I've had no trouble living with that.

That second attempt at a night dive was when we were on Saba, a tiny island southeast of the Virgin Islands. It isn't much more than a volcano rising up out of the Caribbean, but that makes it one of the best diving spots anywhere, with some of the steepest drop-offs. Will loved pushing the limits, and after our first two trips to Grand Cayman, we ended up going there more than anywhere else.

We first heard about Saba from Davide. Will wasn't traveling with Rama the way he had before we met, but Davide still took trips with him. Rama had started traveling to Saba for the diving, and telling all his followers that they had to try it. Will had heard about it, and right before we left for a trip we'd planned to St. Martin — we had picked St. Martin because it was a direct flight; Will hated having to change planes—Davide came back and told us how great Saba was.

From St. Martin, you can actually see Saba, and we decided to take a day-trip to look around. There are two ways to get from St. Martin to Saba. There's a flight that makes the trip in 12 minutes, and a catamaran that takes an hour. We decided to fly, and took the 19-seat Twin-Otter, a special plane made for getting around the parts of the world where they don't have much in the way of airports. It's known for it's ability to take off and land with very little runway, which is fortunate, because Saba has the shortest commercial runway in the world. The first time you see it, you think, "We're going to land on that?" It's surrounded by water on three sides; I'm pretty sure this is what it feels like to land on an aircraft carrier.

It's more than worth it, though, because Saba's one of the most beautiful places in the world. There's not much more than a thousand natives living there, in three or four towns on the mountainside, and the rest is rainforest. We found a wonderful hotel, Willard's of Saba, where there are only eight rooms, and that's where we stayed every time we were there. We became regulars, and after a while, we didn't even bother to make reservations. We'd just show up and say "We'd like our room, please."

That's how Will always operated. He liked to establish relationships with people, and if he couldn't do that, he'd just go somewhere else where he could. Wherever we went, Will got to know people. He'd meet a new person and start right in asking them questions, and everybody likes talking about themselves. But he didn't do that in a premeditated, manipulative, way; he was genuinely interested in just about everybody, really, and knew how to draw anyone out. People remembered us wherever we went because of it.

One of the people we met on Saba, Ted McCoy, became one of our closest friends after we'd been going there a while. We'd usually leave on a Thursday, spend a night on St. Martin, and then take the hop plane to Saba the next morning. When it was time to come home, whatever day we had scheduled for our return, whether it was Sunday, Monday or Tuesday, we'd end up staying just one day more. We called it a case of "just one more day-itis." (We tried to schedule that in, but then we'd end up staying one day more than *that*.)

Ted was working as a dive master for the diving company we were going out with, and after we'd spent three or four trips diving with him, he started coming out with us for a beer after we'd get back to the island. Ted eventually moved back to the South Fork of Long Island, where he'd grown up, but by then we were friends for life. In fact, when Will and I decided it was time to get a house outside of the city, it was Ted's father who found us our place in Sag Harbor, right near where they both lived.

If those first dives off Grand Cayman were beautiful, the diving we did with Ted around Saba were no less than spectacular. Around Grand Cayman, and pretty much all the rest of the Caribbean islands, the gradual slope of the beach continues underwater, sometimes remaining shallow for hundreds of yards out. Because Saba is just a mountain jutting out of the water, there are a steep underwater cliffs all around it. You can be swimming along thirty or forty feet down, and suddenly you look down and there's a thousand feet of deep blue nothing underneath you.

Jutting up out of those fathomless depths are pinnacles and sea mounds that reach up from who knows how far down to within 100 feet of the surface, and they're all covered with different colored corals, and a lot of them are surrounded by dozens of different species of brightly colored tropical fish: squirrelfish, butterflyfish, angelfish, parrotfish, triggerfish, and a dozen others, including all sorts of eels. It was like the reef aquariums Will built, times a hundred.

As soon as we started diving there, Will and I started having underwater fights, because no matter how deep we went, he always wanted to go deeper. Will used to say that he wanted to buy me a yellow wet suit with a red mask and fins, because I was such a "dive chicken," and I used to tell him that he was a terrible dive buddy. You're supposed to have a buddy by your side when you dive, and he'd always end up bailing on me and going deeper than I was willing to go.

That was how Ted became Will's regular diving buddy, and also what got him into technical diving. You can only dive so deep and stay down so long on the air you get in regular tanks. There are very precise and specific formulas about how long you can stay down at what depth, with what amount of oxygen in your blood.; that's one of the things you get tested on when you take the written certification test. If you go past those limits, the oxygen bubbles in your blood will expand on the way up as the pressure around you decreases, and that's what gives you the bends. If you screw up and come up too fast, the first thing you'd do is grab a tank, get back in the water, and sit there for a while at 30 or 50 feet. But if it's more serious, you have to use a decompression chamber, where they raise the air pressure until it balances the oxygen in your blood, and then slowly bring you back to the air pressure at sea level. Not every diving site has access to a decompression chamber, and another reason that Will liked diving Saba is that they do. Which is smart, because on one of our trips, he needed it.

I had come back home early for some reason, no doubt having to do with Tradeware, and Will stayed on a few more days to get in some more diving with Ted. My phone rang at seven in the morning.

"Kerry, it's Ted. The good news is Will's okay. The bad news is he's in a chamber."

Will and Ted had spent the day diving, and when they were done, they'd gone up to Ted's place, which is up the mountain at about 1200 feet above sea level. Will woke up in the middle of the night in agony. Ted called for an ambulance, and they got him right into the chamber. He had to do four four-hour sessions over the next couple of days. During those four hours, you can't do anything but sit there in the chamber, and they had the pressure down to 80 feet, and he said the whole ordeal was painful. Even after that, he had to stay on the island a couple of extra days before it was safe for him to fly, and he was still in pain for another month.

If you want to go down deeper than about 120 feet, besides being very careful about stopping on the way up, you have to change the mix of gasses you're breathing, so you don't end up with dangerous amounts of oxygen in your blood. The other thing you have to do is recirculate your air, so what you can carry in your tanks lasts long enough for you to come back up slowly enough to decompress safely. With a regular scuba (Self-Contained Underwater Breathing Apparatus) setup, which is called open-circuit gear, after you breathe in the air from your tanks, what you breathe out is released into the water. A rebreather is a closed-circuit (or partly closed, depending on the specific system) scuba system that takes the air you breathe, extracts some of the CO_2, injects more oxygen, and then sends it back for you to breathe again. If you're using a rebreather, you don't leave a trail of bubbles, because the air you breathe stays in the system, and you don't run out of air as fast because it all gets reused.

Almost all recreational diving uses open-circuit scuba gear. Technical diving uses rebreathers and different gas mixes so you can go for long, deep dives, and it's essential of you want to go cave-diving--which, frankly, is about the scariest thing I can think of. You're going into total darkness with three lights, and you're moving through restricted passages; it wasn't something I would ever do, but Will loved it. It was all about the complexity and the control for him. What he thought was crazy was mountain climbing, because you have no control. One misstep, and you're dead, and you just couldn't account for every crevice. But with diving, he said, you check your equipment, you know what's going on, you have triple redundancy, and the only thing that could kill you was complacency.

There was never any question that this was the kind of diving that Will wanted to do, and for that he had to get certified on a rebreather. Compared to getting certified for a rebreather, the PADI test we took was as easy as getting a learner's permit at the DMV. You can rent scuba gear anywhere, but they won't even sell you a rebreather if you haven't already taken classes and signed up for the test.

Will decided to train with Leon Scamahorn., who designs rebreathers in Seattle. Most people who train with Leon go to Seattle and Leon trains them there. Will didn't want to train in Seattle, though, so he paid for Leon to come and stay in Saba for a couple of weeks.

What was funny was that Leon was a military guy, and acted like one. He was Will's drill sergeant, and had Will getting up at six a.m. every morning. Will usually stayed up until four or five, and didn't get up before noon, so this was a real rude awakening for him. And then, to get him used to the long dives you make with a rebreather, Leon was making Will stay under water in the pool for what seemed like all day. They became great friends, though. Will later began programming the electronics for Leon's designs, and they relied on him so much that the company stopped producing equipment for a while when he was no longer around.

That was the trip when I became a really good diver, too. I barely saw Will the whole time we were there, so while he was in boot camp with Leon, I would go out every day and dive with Ted and whatever group he was taking out. Because Will wasn't there, I had to learn to rely on myself, which forced me to become a self-sufficient diver.

. With diving, like with anything else, you build up a tolerance, and toward the end of that trip, I swam through the Cathedral, a beautiful coral formation that I never would have tried before. I reached my maximum depth of 176 feet—I couldn't go any deeper than that on air. It was a real triumph for me, and if Will had been with me the whole time, I probably never would have done that. That's also the trip when I went out for a night dive again. Or tried, at least.

After Will got his first rebreather, he started tinkering. It was exactly the sort of thing that really engaged him. Technical diving involved the mechanical engineering of the device itself, the chemistry of mixing two or three gases, the biology of how the body processes the gases, the mathematics of precisely mixing the gases according to all of that, and programming for the dive computers. (Even though I never did any tech diving, just from hanging out with Will, I'm the most knowledgeable recreational diver you'll ever meet. Ask me about bubble mechanics sometime. Will rubbed off on you that way.)

You can still find Will's name all over the internet if you start looking at diving sites, particularly in the Usenet groups where the really serious divers got together to discuss small but pivotal technical matters. Of course, you have to keep in mind that when you're 400 feet down and mixing your own air supply, a tiny technical detail can be the difference between life and death. That's one of the things Will kept saying he loved about it, too. It was a mental challenge; an exercise in control.

Will eventually started designing his own rebreathers, and doing the electronics and programming to improve the designs of others, but what he's best remembered for is Z-plan. Z-plan is an algorithmic program for using trimix (an air supply mixed from three different gases) at various depths. Once he'd written it, he posted it and distributed it for free, and it became the most popular program among tech divers. (The Z is for our cat, Zach.)

There have been new programs since then, but a lot of people still depend on Z-plan, and people in the online diving groups still talk about Will with a certain amount of reverence. He's cited as an authority in all sorts of conversations, and if you dig back far enough, you can see why. Here, for example, is what happened when somebody posted to the alt.rebreather group that he was using hearing aid batteries as O2 sensors in his rebreather.

First, a few of the divers in the group asked the guy some questions, because it seemed unlikely, and then the entire group took sides. The debate went on for weeks. By the time Will joined in, the two groups were polarized. He took a look around, said, "Hold on," went away for a while, then came back and put the whole thing to an end:

> Date: Thu, 19 Mar 1998 00:00:47 -0500 (EST)
> From: "William M. Smithers" <will@tradeware.com>
> Subject: Zinc-Air Test Results.
>
> After the noise on the list about zinc-air cells, and some initial quickie trials I did (which were indecisive, tending toward negative), I decided to give the cells a more thorough evaluation. I did this because if they turned out to work, the small size makes them extremely appealing for use in a bailout rebreather.
>
> *[A bailout rebreather is an small backup system you bring along, just in case something goes wrong; two of Will's rebreather designs started out as bailout systems.]*

For the test, I did a couple of dozen runs in my test pressure pot (totaling over 14 hours of tests, using 5 different cells), using compressed air to create O2 partial pressures of between 0 and 2.6. I used compressed air because it offers more accuracy due to the wider pressure range, and because it also better simulates actual ambient pressure at depth (for a given PO2). Plus, since many batteries are directly affected by pressure, I figured this was a good thing to do.

The depth sensor I used is calibrated for 0-1500fsw, with an accuracy of +-0.25% of full scale range.

These tests are far from what I'd consider exhaustive, but I think they do offer a true feel for the dynamics of the cells.

For the tests, I used Duracell DA13 cells, loaded with a 1k Ohm resistor, and used about a 100fpm descent rate, and a 60fpm ascent rate. The raw millivolt values you see are relative to a constant voltage offset that I applied (something like 1.1v)to get finer-grained results, and reflect (more-or-less) the baseline voltage of a new cell in air. No amplification of the raw output was performed. So the reading is a "differential" voltage between the baseline and the current sensor reading.

The first test was a general linearity and repeatability test, which I performed with various PO2's about a dozen times. For this test, the depth was moved as noted above. After each adjustment, the sensor was given about 10 seconds to settle before the sample was taken. Total time at each depth was typically 20-30 seconds, as this is the time it took to write down the data and start adjusting the pressure. I haven't listed the correlation and error rates here, but feel free to calculate them if you're in the mood.

0 fsw, 16.8mV, .21 PO2
66 fsw, 30.4mV, .62 PO2

130, 37.5, 1.03
214, 58.0, 1.56
365, 67.0, 2.53
217, 34.7, 1.59
131, 32.2, 1.04
66, 26.1, .62
0, 12.9, .21

As you can see, things are looking pretty good on the way down, but something happens on the way back up to screw it up. I ran a bunch of identical tests, and was confused by this, until I figured out what was going on.

Notice that when the sensor gets back to a .21 PO2, it is 3.9 mV below the voltage it was at the start of the "dive." If you add that voltage to the ascending results, your linearity is more-or-less restored. Also, the sensor baseline voltage stays at 12.9 and does not bounce back to the original starting voltage, so the next test run starts at 12.9 at 0fsw. At the end of the next run, you've got an even lower voltage.

After a bunch of runs, I suspected that what was happening is that the cells are tremendously stressed by operating under elevated PO2's, and consequently burn off a large amount of their "vital capacity" under these conditions. Burning off vital capacity translates into a lower output voltage.

I figured that the best way to counter this would be to raise the load resistance, so as to lighten the peak load under high PO2. I used a 5.5k Ohm value.

I did another series of runs, this time diving to a fixed depth and remaining at that depth for a typical bounce dive period. The results were pretty much the same, with the voltage quickly dropping when a depth/PO2 of 1.6 was reached, only the drop rate wasn't as fast.

I raised the resistor value to 10k Ohms, and it improved

things a bit, but not much. Here's a typical run (the pressure adjustments are because my test post seems to lose about 1fsw every few minutes due to leakage):

0fsw, 3.8mV, 8:41 PM
33, 13.2, 8:42
65, 19.1, 8:42
99, 24.5, 8:43
133, 24.3, 8:44
220, 42.6, 8:45
219, 42.6, 8:47
217, 39.5, 8:51
(restored pressure to 220)
220, 39.2, 8:52
219, 37.4, 8:56
218, 36.1, 9:00
217, 35.0, 9:03
216, 33.5, 9:07
215, 33.1, 9:09
212, 31.2, 9:16
211, 29.4, 9:21
209, 29.1, 9:26
(restored pressure to 220fsw)
219, 29.8, 9:27
219, 30.8, 9:29
218, 28.7,, 9:31
217, 27.8, 9:35
216, 27.1, 9:38
214, 26.5, 9:43
155, 18.2, 9:45
155, 18.0, 9:47
132, 16.1, 9:48
132, 15.9, 9:49
99, 14.3, 9:50
66, 6.7, 9:51
66, -7.5, 9:53
33, -15.0, 9:54
33, -17.1, 9:55

15, -21.6, 9:55
0, -27.3, 9:57
0, -28.0, 9:58

As you can see, more of the same. After an hour at an actual PO2 of 1.6, the sensor is reading the equivalent of a 1.1 PO2. If this was running a set-point controller, your PO2 would have been elevated to well over 2.0, as a result of the drift.

Finally, I raised the cell load to 15kOhms, which produced downright nutty results, which I won't bother to reproduce here.

Specifically, it appears that the higher the load value, the lower (and less accurate) the differential voltage response, and the slower the response time. However, the cell does not burn down as quickly at higher resistance.

So, here are my conclusions on small zinc air cells:

[1] They burn off too much of their life under high-oxygen partial pressures to be useful. This burn-rate occurs so swiftly that it creates a high degree of continuously increasing drift. The drift increases so quickly (minutes) that it quickly brings the voltage readings outside of the acceptable error margin.

[2] I suppose it would be possible, with a huge expenditure of effort, to create a drift compensation table, then digitally (or otherwise) apply this table, but I'm not going to bother.

[3] Use of these cells without drift compensation, or for any prolonged period (measured in minutes or hours, depending on PO2 levels), to control or monitor O2 is extremely dangerous, as the cells will begin to show lower-and-lower PO2 readings during the course of a single dive.

The results weren't encouraging enough to continue with

tests for temperature and humidity, as I had planned.

My final note is this: For your own sake, don't take my word for it. If you are really diving these sensors, don't do so again until you've verified these results for yourself, especially with a 1k load, as your life could be measured in minutes if you run a high PO2.

-Will

That was the end of the debate, and that was typical Will. Give him a problem that others talked about, and he'd roll up his sleeves, take something apart or build something, whichever was necessary, and figure it out. And as much as he liked people, he did not suffer fools gladly. You can see why he was so respected in the online community.

(Will wasn't always this serious and businesslike in his online life. He liked to goof around, too, and mess with people, just for fun. There was a notorious instance when he parodied all the earnest participants debating the meaning of Zen in one group, and he also posted this about Zach, of Z-plan fame:

Subject: My cat loves my vibrator

OK, so it's not *that* kind of vibrator, but it made for a catchy tag line.

I was using my muscle massager, when I noticed a gleam of jealousy in the eyes of Zach, my cat. So I figured I would scare him off by giving him a buzz with it; it's a pretty strong, semi-pro massager, and I figured he'd run off. He

LOVED it. Now I come home and find him sitting next to the thing, looking up at me with "pleeeze, pleeeze, pleeeze" eyes. No kidding.

I think the little bastard is hooked.

-Will)

One day during one of our Saba trips, I was feeling a little sick, and didn't go out diving, because you're not supposed to dive when you're stuffed up. I wasn't so sick that I wanted to sit around doing nothing all day, though, so I decided to take a walk up Mount Scenery into the rainforest. I had been having nightmares on and off whenever we stayed on Saba, and when I mentioned it to Will, he told me it was because the vibe was tricky there, just like on Wall Street. Saba was a place of power, a vortex of forces, which is what attracted Rama there in the first place.

I mostly took Will's word on this sort of thing, because he was much more aware of these kind of forces than I was, although I had already had an encounter when we were looking for a place to live in New York. On the day I took the walk, though, I wasn't thinking of any of that. In fact, I wasn't thinking at all, really. I didn't even think to bring water.

I walked up the steps that had been carved into the mountain, and after a while I started to get spooked. It was a sunny day, there was nobody around, but the longer I walked, the more I felt a sense of menace. When I saw *The Blair Witch Project*, I recognized the sense of dread that they developed as the camera tracked through the empty woods. It felt just like that; the rainforest started to take on that same threatening appearance that they captured in the movie.

It was a long walk up, and it kept getting worse and worse. Finally, I thought, "Screw this," and turned around and ran all the way back down to our hotel. I had been walking up for about an hour, but I made it back down in under fifteen minutes. When Will got back from diving that day, I told him what happened, and he said, "I told you the vibe here was tricky."

You'd think an encounter with unseen malevolent forces would make that the worst experience I ever had on an island, but it wasn't. The worst had to be our second trip to Hawaii.

We went to Hawaii three times. The first time was fun; Will and I did some diving, even though the water in the Pacific was so cold that I had to buy a thicker wetsuit. The last time we went, in 1999, we brought Trinity with us and it was a calm, normal, family vacation.

But on our second trip, we ended up staying for almost a month, and there were all sorts of ups and downs. It was August of 1998 and we had planned a two-week trip. The first week was great. It was just me and Will. We went to Mauna Lani Bay and took a tour. We did some shore dives and went to the top of Mauna Kea, had some great meals, and in general had a great time doing all sorts of couple stuff.

The start of the second week was unofficially Will's part of the trip. Will had by then been seriously involved with rebreathers and reef aquariums for a while. He had made a bunch of contacts through the Usenet groups for both subjects, and he'd arranged to get together with some of them while we were there. We flew over to Honolulu for a couple of days, and met up with a bunch of his rebreather people. I hung out with them for a while, but it was like spending time with a bunch of mechanics at a antique car show, with all the hoods up.

Finally, I said, "Okay, boys, that's it for me. Have fun. I'm going shopping." One thing about Will is, whenever we traveled, he didn't pack anything, really, and he always told me not to, either. He'd throw some underwear and socks in a bag, and that would be it. When we got to our destination, the first thing he'd do was go out and buy clothes. That way, he said, he was always dressed right for wherever we were. I kept that in mind for the next couple of hours.

When I got back, Rich Pyle, one of Will's new friends, said, "Why don't we do a dive?"

I didn't know it at the time, but when Rich Pyle says he's going for a dive, it's not the same as when most people say it. Rich Pyle is a coral reef expert at Hawaii's Bishop Museum, and a deep-diving pioneer. He probably knows more than anybody else about what they call "the Twilight Zone." The Twilight Zone is the stretch of coral reefs between about 200 and 500 feet deep. Divers have been exploring reefs down to 200 feet for a long time, and we've been sending bathyspheres down to the ocean floor since the 1930s, but because we didn't have the technology, we really didn't know anything about what was between those two areas. Rich was the first person to start using rebreathers to explore the ecology of the Twilight Zone in a serious way, and he's discovered over 150 new species of fish there.

So, when you go for a dive with Rich Pyle, it's not going to be a nice little recreational dive. We drove over to Diamond Head, where Rich brought us to a rickety little boat. He'd arranged for a real Captain Quint type to pilot the boat (actually, his seventh-grade science teacher; Rich had grown up on Hawaii), and they started loading their rebreathers and tanks into the boat for the dive. I figured I'd just go back to shopping for a few hours, but Will stopped me.

"Where are you going?"

"Shopping."

"No, you can't. The safety diver didn't show up. We need you to come with us."

I protested, but they really wanted to go on this dive, which is how I ended up sitting on that rickety boat for four hours while Will and Rich went down to 400 feet hunting for exotic fish.

As safety diver, I had to stay suited up in the boat, and play out a line as they went down. This was a drift dive, and the currents were different at 400 feet than at the surface, so without that line, we'd have no idea where they were. They sent up a buoy when they got to 400 feet, and at that point, I had to start counting. Whether they caught any fish or not, they could only stay at 400 feet for ten minutes or so before they had to start ascending. About midway through the dive, a storm started to blow in, and the water was getting choppy, so I started worrying about how bad it might get, and feeling generally uncomfortable.

When their time was up, I got in the water with a couple of tanks and took them down to 100 feet, where I clipped them to the mooring line, in case they needed the extra air on the way up. The water was so clear that from there I could see that everything was just fine. Will held up the fish they'd just caught so that I could see it. While a storm was blowing in on the surface, down at 400 feet, things couldn't have been more serene.

The ascent took a full two hours, because they'd been down so deep. When they finally got to the boat, Will showed me Fred and Barney, the two fish that were destined for our aquarium on Wall Street. They were a new species of butterfly fish, and Rich sold the third one they'd brought up to a collector in Japan for $80,000.

On the trip back to the marina, Rich started to feel the telltale tingling in his joints that lets you know you're bent. Rich had been seriously bent in the past, had actually been paralyzed for months, so he wasn't taking any chances. He grabbed a tank and went back down to thirty feet and stayed there until he was sure it was safe to come up. Will, who did the same dive, didn't have any problems that day. I didn't have any decompression problems, but by then I was borderline seasick from the storm.

That night, we went back to Rich's house for a party, and Will was in his glory. One of the guests was Charles Debeek, who was the co-author of *The Reef Aquarium*, which is basically the bible for the reef aquarium crowd. So here was Will getting to talk to the world's foremost reef aquarium expert and the world's foremost deep coral reef expert. They had a great conversation, and Will couldn't have been happier. When we were leaving for the night, Charles and Rich asked what we were doing the next day, and offered to take us on a back-room tour of the Honolulu Aquarium. That's where the real problems with this vacation started.

When we were planning the trip, Will had invited Ralph and Linda, and Bill and Shannon, Bill's girlfriend at the time, to join us. Since Will laid out the money for the tickets and hotels, we were able to schedule the trip so that we had a week for just us, before they got here. We were supposed to be back to Maui to meet them when they arrived that next afternoon. But here were these two world experts with access to everything, offering to take us behind the scenes at the aquarium, a once-in-a-lifetime opportunity.

In the end, we just couldn't pass up the experience, and we got a real insider's look at the workings and holdings of this great tropical aquarium. Rich gave us the fish tour and Charles gave us the coral tour and then they took us to the back of the house to see all the tanks and how the water was cycled. The whole day was fascinating, and then it was suddenly three o'clock, and we to race to the airport as fast as we could to make a flight back to meet everybody.

Now, Ralph and Linda knew that we would be flying back from Honolulu, but they'd said that they were going deep sea fishing that afternoon, so we weren't too worried about getting back late. It just didn't work out, though. They had decided not to go, and everybody was in a bad mood when we arrived, from waiting for us.

The next day things went wrong, too. Ralph and Bill had just gotten certified in Salt Lake City so they could dive with us, so Will had chartered a boat for the six of us to go out diving that day. In the morning, though, Ralph, Linda, Bill and Shannon decided not to go. We had already charted the boat, so Will and I went out by ourselves. We had a great time—we had the whole boat to ourselves, and we got in three great dives—but back on land, the bad moods didn't let up.

That whole week, nothing went right. We spent the first four days in Maui, and then we went to Kauai for the rest of the week, and Linda didn't like any of the places we'd arranged for them to stay. The restaurant back in Salt Lake City wasn't doing too well, so Ralph and Bill were already in a bad place from the start, and it seemed like that was all we talked about. By the end of the week, I didn't want to hear another word about business.

On the last day we all went to the airport together. They were booked on a flight to Salt Lake, and we were flying into JFK.

Their flight left first, so we saw them off, and then Will looked at me and said, "There's no way we're going home. I need a vacation." We canceled the flight and spent another two weeks at the Mauna Lani Bay. It was our most severe case of "just one more day-itis."

Chapter Six

Ruling the World

Even though Will was the person most responsible for getting Tradeware to where it is, he was never really that interested in the company. We're hugely successful, but I always thought that if he had gotten more interested and involved in the business, well, who knows how far we might have gone? But instead, Will put most of his energy into reef aquariums, or testing zinc batteries as O2 sensors and designing rebreathers; things that seized his attention and gave his intellect and his imagination a workout.

I was looking at one of Will's old datebooks, from 1995, and for a few months, day after day is blocked out for IH, with an occasional business meeting mentioned, like an afterthought. There are entire weeks with entries that say nothing but *IH twelve – midnight*, and there are notes like this: *89% directional accuracy…the second pass filter works great!…The weight variable got the directional accuracy to 94+%! Closed the day by running five of the needed stocks thru. August accuracy is over 85%...It will take several hours (like 7) to finish the IH runs tomorrow.*

(There are also notes like *VOYAGER first episode WAS good*. Will loved science fiction, and turned me on to some great books, like *Neuromancer* and *Stranger in a Strange Land*. Of course, instead of just walking into Barnes & Noble like anybody else would have, Will had to find a leather-bound collection of the great science fiction novels. I have to admit that I'm glad to have it now.)

IH stands for Information Harvester, and all those notes and all that time were part of Will's attempt to write a program to predict the market and rule the world. Tradeware had been getting a monthly CD from the NYSE that contained all of their historical information for every symbol on the board. Will figured that if he could ferret out and dissect the patterns in that data, he could use them to predict what would happen next.

He got very excited about it. There was a while when he was sure he was going to get it. I remember him saying "Eighty percent accuracy! We're going to be rich!" I had my doubts, and I didn't hesitate to share them, but it wouldn't have surprised me if he really managed it. If anybody could do it, it would have been Will.

But, finally, Will came into the office one day, looking sort of sheepish. "Um, Kerry?" he said. "We're not going to rule the world. I wasn't getting 80% accuracy. IH was cheating." It turned out that when the program was correctly predicting patterns within the historical data, it was because it had been sneaking looks at the future data the results were going to be measured against. What he'd done was write a very clever and sophisticated program that was capable of predicting the past. I didn't often get a chance to say "I told you so" with Will, but, believe me, I did this time.

While Will was doing that, I had continued writing code to develop FIX compliant servers and systems for our clients. And it wasn't as if Will was *always* out riding motorcycles and building reef aquariums and planning to take over the world. He was the one who would sit down and sketch the architecture of the systems I was coding, and he was still out getting us new clients, like Cantor Fitzgerald.

When it came to selling Tradeware, Will's problem back then was that people were still a little bit afraid of the technology. The traders would ask him "Why do I need this?" when what they really meant was "If I buy this from you, the system will end up automated, and I'm out of a job."

Of course, trading is a relationship business, and now they know that going electronic doesn't eliminate their positions. But at the time, Will wasn't just selling our product, he had to sell the idea of our product, and the FIX standard ended up being an important part of that. He would explain to people why they would want to receive orders electronically from clients, and with FIX he could show them that eventually everyone would be using electronic systems.

We couldn't have been more perfectly set up to be the first vendor to implement FIX. Until then, each trader, on both the buy and sell side, would have either their staff IT people or consultants like us write a system for their internal trafficking of trading information. Each time one of those firms wanted to start trading electronically with another firm, they'd come up against the fact that their systems weren't compatible. They spoke different languages. The FIX protocol was going to be the lingua franca of the financial industry, and we made it the official language of Tradeware; we became the first native speakers.

I got so involved in writing FIX engines that I was constantly on the phone with the two guys who came up with the protocol, Christopher Morstatt of Salomon and Bob Lamoureux at Fidelity Investments. (This was the year that the hot toy to buy for Christmas was "Tickle-Me Elmo," and—when he wasn't around of course—Will started calling Bob "Tickle-Me Lamoureux.") I really sort of became the FIX police, because I was the first vendor implementing the protocol. I'd write something, then call them up to test, and we'd figure out what worked and what didn't. One time I kept running up against the same problem until I figured out what it was. I called up Chris and asked, "Can you start following your own specs, please?"

We were friendly, but I was sort of in awe of these guys, particularly Chris. FIX was a remarkable, industry-changing achievement, and even when we kidded around, I never forgot that. So it was a really big deal when Will got off the phone one day and said "Oh my God. Chris Morestatt is coming here with some guys from Goldman Sachs." Because we were the first vendor to get so deeply involved in FIX, they wanted to come in and see what, exactly, we were doing with it.

It was just a networking visit, but really, it could be much more important than that. We were in the process of becoming a known force in the IT community on Wall Street, and even though this wasn't technically a high-pressure sales call, the impression these guys took away with them could make a real difference in the future of Tradeware. Will decided that nobody needed to know that Tradeware, a company that was making a bid to become the main supplier of FIX-compliant servers and interfaces to the biggest firms on Wall Street, had a staff consisting of two people. As he put it at the time, quoting the movie *A Few Good Men*, "They can't handle the truth."

Will was determined to make a good impression, and he felt that we wouldn't be able to do that unless we had a bigger staff. He was worrying about it, until he suddenly said, "Wait a minute. We live in New York City. New York is full of actors." He got on the phone, made some inquiries, and ended up hiring six actors for two days.

We had the actors come in the day before the meeting so we could prep them for their "show." Will assigned one person to the big reception desk, we told a couple of them to sit at computers and surf the internet, looking as if they were doing something, and had two more just sort of move around the office, looking busy and efficient. The actors, by the way, loved it. They thought it was hilarious.

The next day, we were all ready for the meeting. We'd told security downstairs to keep an eye on who signs in and call us when they got here. When we got the call we announced, "Places, everyone!" and when the elevator doors opened, everyone was in character. The actors pretending to be programmers appeared to be immersed in deep programming conversations, and the receptionist acted just like a receptionist. Will and I hustled our guests into the conference room, and just about everything went perfectly.

It turned out that Chris Morstatt and Will had met in the past. Chris stared at Will for a minute, and said, "Wait, you're *that* Will Smithers! You did Project Blackbird. That was brilliant."

Salomon is known in the financial community as being really great technically, very sophisticated and forward looking, and they'd had Will come in, long before I met him, to do some tricky programming for them. I had always known that Will was brilliant, but here was a guy, Chris Morstatt, that the whole financial community thought was brilliant, and he felt the same way about Will. I was in awe of Chris, and he was in awe of Will.

So, it was no surprise after that, that the meeting went well. The actors did their jobs without a hitch, we were able to talk FIX with them as fluently as they could. We cemented our place in the eyes of IT people from two of the biggest firms on Wall Street that we were going to be the FIX go-to guys.

There was just this one thing. While we were sitting in the conference room, one of the Goldman guys kept looking around at everything, with a curious expression. Finally, he said, "You know, this all looks like Goldman surplus furniture."

It wasn't often that Will got surprised. He usually had a cool response for anything. This time, though, he was as taken aback as I was. He came back pretty quickly, though, and said, "Oh, yeah. We got a great deal on it," and we moved on as though we'd picked everything up through normal channels.

Just as they stepped onto the elevator to leave, having just walked past the new/old reception desk, the same guy from Goldman said, "Why do I feel like a sting is going on here?"

Will said, "I have no idea what you mean," and then the elevator doors closed. Will pulled a roll of bills out of his pocket and paid off our actors.

We never had to do anything like hire actors again, because not long after, within six months of getting here, we got our first really big job in New York. Will signed up Herzog Heine Geduld, the third largest over-the-counter brokerage firm on Wall Street. They were a major presence on the NASDAQ, but now they wanted to move into trading on the New York Stock Exchange. They'd just pulled off a major coup that made everyone sit up and take notice when they hired away the head of the NYSE group of another firm, who brought all his traders with him.

Now they needed a whole new system, and Will had convinced them that Tradeware was the company to do the job. It wasn't just a floor system for the NYSE, either: they were in markets in three other cities, including Boston and Chicago, and we designed new systems for their operations in those markets, too. I have no idea how he landed this deal, but it was worth $600,000, and he came back to the office with a check for $300,000.

Ever since Tradeware started, we'd had business, and we were never in real danger of going under, but at that point, it was pretty much hand to mouth. There were some checks that had to be written right away against that money. There might even have been a few checks that had already been written against that money. Let's just say to that prevent any problems at the bank, the Herzog check had to be deposited as soon as possible. Or a little bit before that.

119

The problem was, we still hadn't switched our account down to New York from the Bank of Boston yet. We'd been doing okay just Fedexing the deposits from New York, but this time, even overnight wasn't going to do it.

Will called from Herzog as soon as he had the check in his hands. (Cue "race against time" music.) I was waiting at the office, all set to go, like the next runner in a relay race. Will got back and I was out the door, heading toward the shuttle from LaGuardia to Boston. If straining forward against your seat belt could make a plane go faster, that flight would have arrived almost before it left.

The teller in Boston must have been familiar with our account, because when she saw the size of the check, she looked up at me and said, "You flew all the way up here just to deposit this, didn't you?"

"I sure did," I told her, "and I'm going back right now." I don't think I was in town for more than 20 minutes.

Will and I had established a rule about deposits: Pay Amex first, then the phone company first, then the rent, and then, if there's anything left over, we'd take care of the other bills. That night, though, after I got back to New York, we went out for a great dinner to celebrate before we did anything else. We agreed that now that we didn't have to worry about bills for a little while we should start to staff up.

Until that point, it had been just me and Will, despite what our visitors saw that day. From then on, we'd be responsible for a real company.

We had a little problem with Herzog not long after this, though, and we almost didn't have any company at all. We immediately started thinking of it as Gray Wednesday.

One night, Will was testing a product of ours called Wave Trader, a basket trading program. Basket trading lets you bundle a group of stocks together, plug in an algorithm that defines how they're handled in relationship to one another, and then deal with the whole "basket" as one thing. Will needed data to run the tests, so he left that day's orders, which had already been executed before the market closed at five, in the system. Unfortunately, he forgot to shut it off when he left for the night, and the next morning, at 9:30, when the Stock Exchange opened, Wave Trader put through that whole day's orders again.

Over at Herzog, they saw what happened right away, and Dave Shekel, the head of the group, called us just minutes after the orders started going through. I immediately got on the phone to "dot services" at the Stock Exchange. That's the office where they process the human interactions that go along with electronic trading. It's all women handling the calls, so Will and I called them the dot services ladies.

I told them what was happening, but by this point, at around a quarter to ten, most of the trades had already gone through. We'd shut it off at this end and stopped a few, but that was it. I asked the dot services lady if she could cancel the orders, but she said that they'd already been sent down to the floor and it was out of her hands. She put me on hold for a couple of minutes, and that's when I suppose I lost my temper a little, because what I said next wasn't exactly polite. "Don't you have some peon there that can run down to the floor and do this?"

Of course, she and the rest of the dot services ladies would be the people I was talking about, and she didn't receive this very well. "I'm sorry, ma'am, but I can't help you," she said, and that was the end of the conversation. When the smoke had cleared, we had committed our client to a four million dollar position that they hadn't asked for.

Will and I looked at each other and had the same thought. "Oh, well. That's it. Tradeware was fun, wasn't it?" We figured it was all over for us. We were toast.

Over at Herzog, Dave was taking it better than we were. He even teased us about it, and said he was surprised we had answered the phone at all—he had expected up to be on our way to the Caribbean by then, to go into hiding.

By ten o'clock there was nothing left for us to do but wait, while Herzog tried to divest four million dollars in stocks nobody had ordered. We were both pretty freaked out, but I went into my office and got right to work on fixing Wave Trader so that would never happen again. As the day went by, Will would come into my office whenever he got a progress report from Herzog. "Its down to three million…now it's two million…they only have a million left to sell." Finally, after lunch, around one or two o'clock, it was down to two hundred and fifty thousand dollars. If we had to pay that, we wouldn't be making any money for the next five years, but at least it was a number we could grasp. We started to relax a little.

It kept going down, and when the market finally closed, Will came and stood in my office door. What was it going to cost us?

Even though I knew at that point that it wouldn't be enough to ruin Tradeware, it wasn't like it was a good thing.

"Well?" I asked him.

'Twelve hundred dollars," he said.

"Oh my god. That's great. They only lost twelve hundred dollars?"

Will laughed. "No, Kerry. They *made* twelve hundred dollars."

So, things turned out alright with Herzog, but because I made that phone call earlier in the day, the Exchange was aware of what happened. Will and Dave Shekel had to go down there and explain what the hell happened. There was some kind of investigating committee, which Will described to me as operating along the lines of the Inquisition.

Will told them it was human error, though, and that I'd written a date-check function into the software that would prevent that from ever happening again. (Which is fortunate, as it saved our asses on another occasion.) After he'd explained that to their satisfaction, they said, "Okay. Fine. Now what about this?" and they played a tape of me on the phone referring to the employees of the Stock Exchange as "peons." Apparently, they were taping when they had me on hold, too, because Will reported that there were a few other less than complimentary phrases that they were having a problem with.

Will told me that he thought I'd been remarkably restrained given the circumstances, but the Exchange was more concerned about the tape than the four million dollar error we'd made. Will apologized repeatedly, but he was told that the dot services ladies were very upset, and when he got back, he said we were going to have to do something.

They still talk about what Will ended up doing.

Every day for a week, he sent the dot services ladies five flower arrangements. My birthday was right around then, and Will sent me one, too, so I know how huge these things were. They more like bushes than flower arrangements, and really, they were more like trees than bushes. When the petals started falling off the one that I had, my office looked like Central Park in the fall.

A week or two later, some upper-level person from the Exchange called to say thank you. He told Will that he'd made the ladies very happy, and that the whole place was buzzing about what he'd done, because it was so outrageous. Will had taken a huge problem and completely turned it around. After that, there was nobody who worked at the Exchange that hadn't heard of Will Smithers and Tradeware.

KERRY SMITHERS

Chapter Seven

Will, Cody, and What Went On Out West

A couple of the new employees we hired after Will got the contract with Herzog came from X-Ticket. Do you remember Will's cult friend Davide? We were staying in his apartment when we first came to New York, because he was on a trip to Korea. Well, the thing is, we had to bootstrap the company from Day One. When we first leased the office at 99 Wall, we didn't have any cash, and the realtor wanted four or five month's rent up front. I had great credit, but my condo was still on the market and I was cash poor. Since all the money that came in to Tradeware went back into the business or paid our living expenses, Will had no money either, and he had no credit at all.

In part, Will had no credit rating because of habitual Rama stuff: staying invisible and moving around. But the time he just walked away from a rented Mercedes when it broke down, leaving it on the side of the road, might have had something to do with it, too.

Davide, on the other hand, whom Will had known for a while, at least since they'd been roommates out in California, had lots of cash, but he had no credit either, probably because he was a Rama person, too. He was just starting up a new company, X-Ticket, and he had money coming in from consulting. He needed an office, too. Between his cash and my credit, we got the office. But X-Ticket went under pretty soon, and we ended up hiring a programmer, David Eaves, who had been working for X-Ticket.

David Eaves was a Ph.D. economist, but we hired him as a developer to maintain the Wave Trader program that got us in so much trouble on Gray Wednesday. It wasn't really his thing, and he didn't last that long, about a year, but we liked him a lot, and Will had a great time talking to him about all sorts of abstract, intellectual subjects. Eaves was about seven years older than us, a Deadhead, and a real character. I called him Glum because he was always so gloomy and pessimistic about everything. No matter what we proposed, Glum would say, "We can't do that. It'll never work." That was part of why we got a little worried when he disappeared on the day Jerry Garcia died.

After three days passed with no word from David, the elevator doors opened and there he was, looking like hell. He obviously hadn't shaved or showered in days, and he looked like his best friend had died, which, in a way, I guess is what happened. He was never really the same after that. He left here for a job at Cantor Fitzgerald, but we stayed in touch, and he kept saying how much he missed California. We encouraged him to move back there, and late in the summer of 2001, he did.

Another person we hired when Davide went out of business was Kurt Philips. Kurt had been Davide's office manager, and now that we were staffed up enough to have an office requiring management, we took him on. He convinced us to hire his boyfriend, Stephen Wong, as our bookkeeper. Stephen had also lost his job when X-Ticket went under. We now suspect we know the reason it happened at all.

As smart as Will was, I guess we were both pretty naïve about people. It didn't occur to us not to trust these guys, until the day we got a letter at home from our accountant, when Kurt and Stephen had been working for us for about two years. Our accountant had been trying to get in touch with Will at the office, but we discovered that if our office manager, who answered the phone and opened the mail, didn't want us to know something, we never heard about it. Kurt had been throwing up roadblocks for weeks.

Our accountant had sent us the records from Tradeware's checking account, with dozens, hundreds of checks made out to cash highlighted. Kurt and Stephen had embezzled something like $80,000 from us over the previous six months or so. Will had authorized Kurt to write checks up to $3000, and he'd gotten right to it. When we went back through the books, we found check after check made out to cash: $300, $500, $200, $500, $700. Kurt would write them and Stephen would cash them. He got really bold towards the end — in one month, he stole something like $15,000.

This was particularly frustrating because Will and I weren't drawing checks through all of this, to make sure we could meet our payroll. We've never missed one, but at times we had to go without paying ourselves, just dipping into the till to keep us going. One year, I think Will showed $10,000 on his W-2. But now we were legit, and it still seemed to be getting harder and harder to pay our expenses. And every morning, there was Kurt, "Good morning, Kerry. Hi, Will," while he was stealing everything he could from us.

We found this out on a weekend, and Will sort of jumped the gun. Instead of keeping quiet until we walked into the office on Monday, or calling the police first, Will called up Kurt at home and, well, let's just say he shared his feelings. By the time the police got to his apartment, Kurt had already taken off, for Florida as it turned out.

We looked into things a little further, and found out he was running a business out of his home on our tab, some kind of gay escort service. It turns out we bought him a computer and a bunch of office equipment, and if all that wasn't bad enough, the computer was a Mac.

In the end, Kurt just wasn't that smart. After a month had passed, he figured the heat would be off and it was safe to come back to New York. A detective was waiting and arrested him on the spot. He went straight to Riker's Island. He sat there for three months because he couldn't raise bail.

When the case finally came to court, we had all the evidence we needed, including a two-inch stack of cancelled checks made out to cash, but because this was New York and all the jails are full, he didn't get sentenced to serve any more time, even though he'd stolen enough money to make it a felony many times over. During the sentencing, the judge made it very clear that if this had been anywhere else, Kurt would have done serious time.

He was supposed to make restitution, but we knew we'd never see any of it, and we didn't. In the end, though, Will figured three months in Riker's was punishment enough for a gay office manager in his forties. We did have a surprise waiting for him, though. We filed his previous year's salary as 1099 income, instead of on a W2. The IRS was going to want to have a word with him.

We ended up hiring four or five people for our first real staff. To take some of the sales pressure off of Will, we hired a salesman right away. Maybe we were a little too eager to do that, because as far as we could tell, he turned out to be the worst salesman who ever lived. It wasn't just that he didn't put any effort into going out and getting business for Tradeware, after a while, he didn't even answer the phone when it rang. This was a salesman who didn't even bother to make sales when they came to him.

That's how Cody Callihan came to be part of Tradeware and part of our lives. Cody had been working as a bond trader in Boulder, Colorado, and wanted to become a trader in New York. He had come to New York and gone to interviews with everybody who would meet with him. It wasn't a good time for bond trading, though, and he couldn't even get a job sweeping leaves for Morgan Stanley.

There was a headhunter Cody was working with who had been cold-calling Will for a while, and this was the first time Will had taken his call. Will said he was looking for somebody with sales background who knew trading. The headhunter told Cody about the job, and even though he insisted that he wanted a trading job and not a sales job, Cody came in to meet with Will.

When Cody walked into the Will's office, Will was sitting and smoking a cigarette with his feet up on his desk. Cody sat down. Will didn't say anything, so Cody didn't either. Finally, Will swung his feet down from the desk, put out his cigarette, and asked, "What kind of tie is that?" Cody's a pretty smart guy, but for a first question, Will had come up with one he couldn't answer. He'd borrowed the tie, and had no idea. But then Will asked him about his experience, and Cody filled him in. When Cody was done, Will asked him about his sales background. Cody had no sales background.

"I'm not a salesman," Cody said. "I don't want to *be* a salesman."

Will had for some reason become convinced, though. Cody was going to come to work for him.

Will said, "Look, you don't know anyone in the city, do you? Why don't you work here for one year, you'll meet every head of trading in the city, and when you get your trading job, you leave with my blessing."

Cody thought about it for a minute, and said he'd be right back. He flew back to Colorado, gave away whatever he wasn't bringing with him to New York, and he's been with us ever since. Cody became an important part of Tradeware, and both Will and I came to trust his judgment about the business. More importantly, though, Cody became Will's best friend.

It wasn't long before we established a regular pattern for the work day. Will still didn't keep anything like regular business hours, so Cody and I would be there all day, and Will would come in sometime in the afternoon. Will still sometimes went to meetings with Cody and made presentations, and he usually dazzled the clients, but Cody learned that whenever Will got involved in a project, or even started reading a really good book, he might end up having to handle a scheduled meeting solo. If Will started a book, he sat and read it until he was done, and that meant that a lot of higher-ups who were expecting to meet him, didn't.

Fortunately, Cody soon learned enough about Tradeware and our products that he could handle things, but one meeting, he really felt it was really necessary that Will show up. Cody went to the client's office, and ten minutes before the meeting was scheduled, Will still hadn't shown up. Cody got on the phone, and told Will, "I don't care what you're doing, this is a huge account. Get over here."

Cody started the meeting, and fifteen minutes into it, Will walked in…wearing a T-shirt that read "Got Wine?" The T-shirt even had a wine stain on it. Of course, once he started talking, Will impressed the hell out of everybody, but this was the sort of thing Cody learned to expect. He never begrudged Will his quirks, though, because he immediately saw the organization that the two of us had created from nothing, and understood the work that had gone into it.

Sometimes Will didn't show up until it was time to leave the office, but we almost always went out for drinks afterward, usually at Bayard's or St. Maggie's Café. Cody and I would do a brain dump, and download everything Will needed to know. Drinks often turned into dinner, but sometimes, especially after Trinity was born, I'd go home straight from the office, and Will and Cody would go out and talk until late. What Will and Cody talked about most, Cody told me, was the future.

What they were going to do next, how Tradeware was just a stepping stone to bigger things. Tradeware produced incredibly complicated software that only had a few potential customers, Will would say. This is clearly not the way to go, if you have a choice. Will envisioned a product that would let him rule the world, some shrink-wrapped software box that everybody in the world would want to buy.

They also talked about the past, and Will told Cody lots of stories. Between us, we were able to piece together a better chronology of Will's "adventures" out West, when Rama probably had something to do with his decisions about where to go. Coincidentally, he'd been in Boulder, Colorado, where Cody came from. He was there for a different reason, though.

When the movie *Good Will Hunting* came out, about a mathematical genius who worked as a janitor at a university, where he hung out solving multidimensional equations in the mathematics department, Will got a call from somebody who had known him them. "Will, you have to see this movie. It's your story."

The University of Colorado at Boulder is the home of a branch of CRI, the Cray Research Institute. Cray is the maker of Cray supercomputers, which, for most of the last thirty years, have been the most powerful computing machines in the world, and there were a number of them at CRI.

How Will got there, why he went there, I guess I'll never know (although I do know that Rama was sending people out to various campuses to recruit followers around then), but I know that Will was a member of the University community in the mid-eighties. I don't know if he was working there, or had friends who worked there, or taught there or were enrolled there, but for some reason, he had an account that allowed him time on the Crays. Now that everybody has a computer, and a decent Palm Pilot is more powerful than the machines NASA used for the first moon landing, it's easy to forget how valuable computer time used to be. Processing power on a machine like a Cray back then was a precious resource, and it was not doled out to just anyone. For some reason, though, the people in charge of who got time on the Cray gave Will an account.

I don't know what he did with his account, either, but it was probably the best toy he'd ever gotten his hands on, and I can imagine him sitting there at the keyboard, grinning at all the computing power he had to play with.

Now, I know this had to have been sometime in 1985 or 1986, and here's how I know that. Will had been at Bell Labs before this, back in New Jersey. Bell Labs was the research and development branch of Bell Telephone, started back when it was a communications monopoly and had more money than God. Over the years, researchers working at Bell came up with things like the transistor, UNIX, information theory, and radio astronomy, so it was no surprise to me to hear that Will had gravitated there. Will had mentioned to me that he was working at Bell Labs when Bjarne Stroustrup the developer of C++, handed out his first paper on the programming language, and that was in September of 1984. And I know that Will was back in New York by 1987, because of something I read in a book.

Liar's Poker is Michael Lewis's book about his experience in the bond trading department at Salomon Brothers. At one point, he mentions in passing some "rocket scientists" that the company had brought in to design an advanced bond-trading system. Remember Christopher Morstatt from Salomon Brothers, the guy who came up to Tradeware and recognized Will? Well, that's why. Will was one of those guys.

In the time between when Will left Boulder and came back to New York to work for Salomon Brothers, he was in California and New Mexico. He was working at Los Alamos at some point, because that seems to be where he got recruited for Salomon Brothers. Los Alamos National Laboratory is where they developed the first nuclear bomb, and Trinity is the name of the site in the desert where they exploded it. Will always insisted that that was the inspiration for our daughter's name, but I swear to you that we decided on Trinity after we saw *The Matrix*. (Trinity, honey, listen to your mother. You're not named after a nuclear bomb.)

In California, Will was apparently a member of a group of people who met every Wednesday night at a Korean restaurant. It was a sort of Algonquin Round Table of software industry geniuses, including Bill Joy, of Sun Microsystems, and Steve Jobs and Steve Wozniak. Again, I don't know how Will made these connections, whether it was Rama stuff or not, but he seems to have known a lot of people. At one point, he was working on virtual reality stuff with Jaron Lanier at VPL Laboratories, and he told both Cody and I about a late night drive to the border with Jaron and Timothy Leary. They were in Jaron's car, and it was so beat up that you could see the road going by beneath your feet. It broke down before they made it all the way there, and they had to abandon it and turn back.

It would make sense if there was some Rama connection involved in all of this, because Will, and lots of other Rama followers, were focused on programming early, and they started a lot of software companies. That was what Rama told them to do, and that's where he got his money. I know that Davide, who shared the office at 99 Wall Street with us, was Will's roommate when he lived in California, but I have no way of knowing how much of a part all that played in this.

In fact, by 1998, the company was growing and everything was going well, and even though Will still occasionally pulled out his tuxedo when he was summoned to a dinner, it was never more than a couple of times a year. I thought Rama was pretty much out of our lives, when I thought of him at all.

Chapter Eight

Ends and Beginnings

One day in April of 1998, I walked into the office and found Will already there. I don't think I'd ever seen him looking as somber as he did then. I knew something bad had happened. I was afraid somebody in the family had died, and in a sense, I was right.

Will had just found out about Rama.

Rama, Frederick Lenz, had been living in a mansion on the Long Island Sound. He had been growing increasingly isolated and paranoid, and he had cut himself off from all but a few of his followers. On April 11, he made a suicide pact with his date for the weekend, a former student of his, took a huge overdose of Valium and drowned off the pier behind his house. (The woman he was with, Brynn Lacey, recovered.) Will told me that Rama had been sick for years, and believed that he took his own life because he had terminal cancer.

Rama's death had two major consequences in our lives. The first was emotional. Although Will never acknowledged it, I think that his teacher's death threw him into a depression that lasted until right before the end. In fact, I think of Rama's death as the beginning of the end of our life together. There were still some wonderful times and huge events ahead for us, but in retrospect, it almost looks like the beginning of the third act of the movie. Rama's death would color everything that happened to us after.

The other thing that happened because of Rama's death was ultimately less important, but a lot more complicated at the time. Shortly after Rama died, we found ourselves in a legal battle for the ownership of our own company. What's most bizarre about it is that one of the bad guys of this story is the National Audubon Society, which is not how you'd usually think of them.

What happened was this. Rama was a very rich man when he died. His estate was worth around 18 million dollars. His will was ambiguous, though, and it led to a big legal battle. On one side was Norman Marcus, who was Rama's accountant and executor. He'd been with a Big Five accounting firm in L.A. with lots of high-profile clients before he quit to handle Rama's interests full-time. On the other side was the National Audubon Society. Rama's will had been drawn up four years before, and it said that his estate should go to a foundation to spread American Buddhism, but only if he'd taken "significant steps" to set up the foundation before he died. Otherwise, everything was supposed to go the Audubon Society.

Shortly after Rama died, Marcus filed documents creating the Frederick P. Lenz Foundation for American Buddhism and the Audubon Society sued. They went at each other in court, but from where we sat at Tradeware, it didn't matter who won, because we received notice that the estate was claiming 50% of Tradeware. Next we got a bill from them for 1.5 million dollars, which was the number they came up with for Will's back dues and half of Tradeware's revenues from 1994 through 1998. Apparently, Marcus wasn't going to honor the verbal agreement Rama had made with Will.

Once again, it looked like Tradeware was in big trouble. We couldn't take a 1.5 million dollar hit. I don't even know how they came up with that number, because they'd never seen our books, and we weren't making that much money yet. Now that Rama was dead, though, Will was ready to fight. "Screw this," he said, and we hired our own high-profile law firm, Brian Cave.

We ended up settling with Marcus for $70,000. That's a lot of money, and I still can't tell you how we managed to come up with that much, because we didn't borrow, but we knew at the time that it was the best deal we'd ever get in our lives. Half of Tradeware for $70,000 was a bargain; technically, that investment is now worth $20 million. The day we settled, Will walked into the office and wrote out two stock certificates for Tradeware, making the two of us the sole owners.

Will's depression through all of that was obvious to me, so I suggested we take a trip to cheer him up. That's when we took the second Hawaii trip, the one with his family. Another thing happened on that trip that I didn't mention yet.

Will and I had been together for six years at this point, and although we might as well have been married, actually *getting* married wasn't something we talked about. Will always insisted that women — including me — were brainwashed by society into thinking they needed a man, but they really didn't. It wasn't an issue for me, though. Our situation was as okay with me as it was with him, but for different reasons. I had already been married, and I was closer to Will than I had ever been to my husband, so as far as I was concerned, a wedding would have been nice, but it would have been beside the point. I didn't need anything on paper to tell me we were a couple. We just were.

For Will, though, it was a bigger thing. Will wasn't like anyone else I'd ever known, and that was the great thing about him. Everything he did, it had to be different, and better, than what everyone else did. But if that was the great thing about him, it was also the biggest problem. It wasn't that he just liked to try to be different, he *had* to be; it was important to him not to be like everyone else, and it threatened to get in the way of him enjoying what was right in front of him. The whole idea of normality was anathema to him, and the last thing he wanted out of life was the whole wife-kids-white-picket-fence deal.

I knew that just like marriage, kids were not on the list of thing that Will wanted to do. I was 37, though, and I was really starting to feel like Marisa Tomei in the scene in *My Cousin Vinny*. My biological clock was ticking. Loudly. I went along with Will on just about everything else, but there were still two of us and there were some things that would just have to be my decision. So, while we were in Hawaii, I announced to Will that it was time for us to have a baby, and that I was going to stop taking my birth-control pills.

"Oh, really?" Will was not pleased.

I made it clear that I wasn't budging, though, and Will realized that it was inevitable. He finally said, basically, "Have a kid. Fine. But it's *your* kid." If we were going to do this, he wasn't changing any diapers, he wasn't getting up in the middle of the night, and he didn't intend to do any of the other things that come with having a child. He would provide the sperm and he would support it, but other than that, I was going to be on my own.

It was a deal I was willing to live with. Of course, I was secretly hoping he'd come around.

He asked me how long he had and I could almost hear the "tick, tick, tick," in his head. Now, at my age, after having been on the pill for a long time, I assumed it would take a while, but you know what happens when you assume.

Five months later, just before Christmas, Will was in Florida, cave-diving with Ted. Cave-diving was his thing lately, and it scared the hell out of me. I remember I told him, half-joking, how mad I was going to be at him if he got himself killed, but it wasn't really a joke. That was when I first started to have premonitions of something bad happening to him. But nobody can stop Will from doing what he wants, and he was having a great time, and that was what he was doing when the stick turned blue. I called him up.

"Will. The stick turned blue."

"Oh," he said. He couldn't have sounded less enthusiastic. "I thought you said this was going to take a long time."

From then on, Will liked to joke about how I'd trapped him, because he thought he had at least another year before he became a father.

After I'd told my family that I was pregnant, my mother asked Will if he was getting excited, and he didn't show any more enthusiasm than he did when I first told him about it. He wouldn't even pretend to be excited for my family. He told my mother that he was afraid the kid would be dumb. My mother looked from Will to me and back again an told Will, "The one thing I can guarantee is that this child will not be stupid."

It was a few months later, in February, that we got some bad news. As long ago as when we were living in Boston, Will had been complaining about an itch on his back. I'd been telling him to see a doctor, and sometime after we found out I was pregnant, I noticed that I could feel something under his skin. Finally, he had gotten a referral to a dermatologist.

The doctor looked and immediately decided he needed a biopsy. Will scheduled it, and we weren't too worried because the doctor was pretty sure it was benign. When the results came back, though, it wasn't. It was XXXXXXX, an extremely rare form of slow-growing skin cancer. (Will, of course, couldn't get just any skin cancer. He had to get special skin cancer.) Will always used to say that you get sick when your energy is down, and following the death of Rama, Will's energy was as down as I'd ever seen. And the next thing, he has cancer.

As it turned out, the itching wasn't a symptom of the cancer at all; the tumor must have been pressing on a nerve, which probably saved his life. XXXXXX has a high mortality rate if it goes undetected and in most people, it just quietly grows to the point that it metastasizes. Even though Will had been putting this off for years, surgery at this stage had a really good survival rate, around 90-95%.

Still, it was scary. Not much scared Will, but he was scared as he went into surgery, and I was, too. Somehow, though, knowing that I had a baby growing inside me helped offset the fear.

The doctors performed what's called Moh's surgery. It's used a lot for cancer on the face, or anywhere else that they particularly want to avoid taking away too much healthy tissue. Instead of just going in and scooping out the tumor, they take slices of skin and put them under a microscope. They keep on taking slices until the reach a slice that has no malignant cells. Will was awake for it, and said he felt like a guinea pig, because there were a bunch of interns, who'd never encountered XXXXXX in there watching.

The surgery was successful, and a year later, when he went if for a follow-up, there were no traces of the cancer at all.

When I was five or six months pregnant with Trinity, I went to Boston to see my family. Will very seldom came with me when I went on trips to see my family—in fact, most of my extended family never had a chance to get to know Will—so I would just go by myself, or later, with Trinity. On this trip, my mother suggested we go look at the baby stores. I said it was too early, which it wasn't, of course, but I was superstitious about it. My mother insisted we were just going to look, though, so, I said, Sure, let's go look.

Up until now, when I thought about what life would be like with Trinity, I thought of having a little person in my life, and what our new family would be like, or how we would watch her grow up. I hadn't really thought about *accessorizing*. Like most new parents, I hadn't realized how much there was to buy. When I got to the store and looked around it really hit me. A new baby needs an incredible amount of stuff.

When I got back to New York I was feeling an entire new category of pressure associated with the baby. Now, I wouldn't say that I grabbed Will by the collar and screamed, "Where are we going to put the *CRIB*? Where are we going to put the *STROLLER*?" but I did manage to convey a sense of urgency. We started looking for a bigger apartment immediately.

We looked at a bunch of places, but in the end, we stayed in Battery Park City. Since our first apartment there, we'd already moved once, into a larger place, a two-bedroom. (Cody and his girlfriend eventually moved into our old place, since we still had time to go on the lease.) Now we moved into 39A at 200 Rector Street, a gorgeous three bedroom, three bath apartment with spectacular views of the Statue of the Liberty and New Jersey and the World Trade Center; it was the beginning of July, 1999.

Our first apartment had been too small to do anything but live in it, and in the second one, half the living room had been Will's workshop, filled with all sorts of tools and gear for diving and aquariums and whatever else had caught his interest, so this was the first time we had a big, beautiful space to live in. Will said, "If we're going to do this, let's do it right," and we set out to decorate the apartment.

Or, I should say, Will set out to decorate the apartment. Will always had an amazing sense of style, whether he was choosing the décor for the reception area of Tradeware and picking out the paintings to hang there, or just buying his own clothes. When I first met him in Boston, he was wearing $1800 suits, and wore his hair slicked back (which I'd never seen anyone do outside of a movie), and later, he had Zegna come to the office to measure him for a shirts and suits. In the morning, he'd stand in front of a mirror deciding between silk ties, and ask me, "Which one's snappin', Kerry?" He was meticulous. The truth is, even though he'd hate the term, Will was a real "metrosexual."

So, when it came to the apartment, Will didn't hesitate. He seemed to know exactly what to do. We went out to ABC and bought some cool oriental rugs, and then we went to Ethan Allen for furniture. Will picked out everything. He wanted a sort of contemporary French style and we walked through Ethan Allen with a saleswoman, while Will pointed and said, "We'll take that, and that, and that, and that." Once we were done, we sat down to pick out fabrics. I could barely picked out the colors to paint our walls, but when the saleswoman brought out the sample book, Will unerringly went to things that looked really good together, beautiful fabrics that worked for our new home.

At one point, Will went off to get a drink of water, and the woman said, "He's amazing! He's got such a great sense for combining colors and textures. Not many men know what they want."

That was Will. He always knew exactly what he wanted. It's just that he didn't know that he wanted a child until I explained it to him.

According to my doctor, he was scheduled to get one on August 24th, shortly after we finished furnishing the apartment.

When no baby arrived on August 24th, the day I was due, Dr. Holland told me come into the office the next day for an ultrasound. When the results showed a nine or ten pound infant who seemed perfectly content to stay where she was, despite getting the first signals from my body that it was time to come out, the doctor decided to induce labor the next day. She told us to be there at seven a.m.

We woke up on the morning of August 26th to a freak summer storm. Everybody knows that as soon as it starts raining in Manhattan it becomes impossible to get a cab, but it wasn't just raining that day, it was raining so much that 10th Avenue, the West Side Highway and the FDR were all closed, which might be the only time that ever happened. Traffic all over New York was an incredible mess, and the subways were flooded, too, so even though we had arranged for a car to pick us up at 6:30 in the morning, it was close to ten before it got there.

The ride up was terrible. Columbia-Presbyterian is all the way up at 166th street, and we were traveling from Battery Park City, which is about as far away from the hospital as you can get and still be in

Manhattan without actually standing in the Hudson River. It took close to an hour of creeping through traffic, driving through flooded streets. I was so anxious that I thought I was having contractions. The cab driver had the radio set to 1010 WINS, the local news station everyone listens to do for traffic reports, and when we heard that a woman had given birth in a car on 105th Street, I was convinced that I was about to become the next local interest story.

The minute we got to the hospital, my contractions stopped, so they were definitely just from nerves. Dr. Holland was waiting for us upstairs, sitting with some other doctors. She'd been concerned, but now that we had arrived, she said, "All right. Let's go have a baby."

I was hooked up to an IV and heart monitors for me and the baby. They started the drugs that induced labor, and I could see on the heart monitor whenever I had a contraction, but it was very strange because I didn't feel anything. It almost feels like I never went through labor because the whole process was so removed and artificial. I'd been reading up on natural childbirth while I was pregnant, and I'd always planned to do it that way: no drugs, no IV, no forceps. But of course, there's nothing natural about inducing, and once that decision was made, the whole natural childbirth idea was out the window.

It was about 11 o'clock when we started, and after a while the doctor decided that I was far enough along to move into a delivery room. We were on the seventh floor, and since we'd gotten there, Will had been going all the way downstairs to have a cigarette about once an hour. Around three o'clock, he decided to go have a cigarette and get something to eat. I hadn't had anything to eat either, but between the drugs and labor, I had no appetite.

While he was gone, of course, is when my water broke and the contractions really started in. I was standing there when I heard a pop, and the baby's heartbeat on the monitor flatlined. I called for a nurse, and fortunately, it was all normal. We both looked at the puddle of the water on the floor and I said, "I think my water just broke." The nurse said, "It certainly looks that way, doesn't it, dear? Now why don't you get back into bed?"

Now, though, I was in serious pain because the contractions were much more intense, and as soon as Will came back, I told him I was ready for an epidural. Will joked with me about the natural childbirth I had talked about all along, giving me sort of a hard time about turning to drugs, but he was funny, and it got me through the half hour it took them to get me set up with the epidural. When they did, it was an immediate relief, from extreme pain to pain at all. Suddenly there was a big goofy smile on my face, because I was so delighted that the pain was gone. "I guess it must be working," Will said, and took a picture of me like that.

For the next six hours, I could tell when I was having contractions, but I couldn't feel them. I got out the book I'd brought, and then we waited it out. I was reading The Memoirs of Cleopatra, by Margaret George, which was one of the big books that summer, but it was also just a big book, almost 1000 pages long. At one point, Dr. Holland came in, saw the size of what I was reading, and said, "Kerry, I know I told you to bring a book to read while we're waiting, but really, it's not going to take that long."

Dr. Holland also told Will to take off his jacket. It was August, and it was hot, but Will had come to the hospital nattily dressed in a nice white shirt and a sports coat. They'd met a few times before, and got along really well, so she started giving him a hard time about how he was dressed. "You might want to take off that jacket, Will...Will, take of the jacket...Will, you're making the rest of us hot. Why don't you take off the jacket?" After a while I joined in, and it went on all through labor, until I was screaming between contractions, "Take off the goddamn jacket, Will!"

Around 8 o'clock, after I'd been in labor for nine hours, I started to feel like I was ready to start pushing and I knew the baby was coming soon. Unfortunately, Dr. Holland had left the room a few minutes earlier. I don't know if it was because of the weather, but a lot of women were going into labor ahead of schedule that day, and she'd gotten a called away to help somebody else.

So, Dr. Holland was busy elsewhere, and I was ready, and it was all starting to hurt a lot, so the nurses gave me some anesthesia to delay me a bit. Unfortunately, that screwed up everything. I found out later from Will that when the doctor came back and found out what had happened, she got very mad and took the nurses out into the hall to yell at them for screwing up.

We tried pushing, but it wasn't working, so the doctor decided to wait another half hour to give the anesthesia time to wear off. But even when she came back, I was having a hard time, and spent another three hours in painful, pushing labor. It was the hardest thing I've ever had to do, but the doctor was adamant about not doing a C-section, so we kept at it.

Finally, sometime after 11, the doctor told Will, I really think you should take off your jacket because it's about to get a little messy in here. It went on for a while more, but eventually, I gave one final push, and Trinity was born, at 11:56. She'd made it just before midnight. She was 8 pounds 6 ounces, and I couldn't believe how big she was. She looked like a giant baby to us, but a giant perfect baby. After they'd cleaned her up and did a quick exam to make sure everything was okay, they left me and Will alone with her, and I felt like she was smiling at us.

Chapter Nine

Fatherhood, Family and Home

About three weeks after we brought Trinity home from the hospital, I told Will I had to go out to get some things for her. Will had never been alone with his daughter yet, and I thought it was time. I said I'd be about twenty minutes, but it was closer to an hour by the time I got back. I'd left them in the living room together, Will reading a book, Trinity in her little baby rocking chair not far away.

When I got back, I walked in, and they were just where I'd left them, but like any new mom, I had to make sure everything was okay.

"Is she okay?"

"Yeah, of course," Will said, without looking up.

"Did you change her?"

"Hell, no I didn't change her. I told you. I'm not changing any diapers."

The poor little thing, I thought. She needed to be changed about every five minutes.

I hurried and put everything down, and took Trinity into her room and put her on the changing table. I opened her onsie her diaper was on backwards. So I changed her diaper, got her dressed again and went out to Will in the living room.

"Wow, Will. You didn't have to change her the whole time I was gone?

"I told you. You wanted a kid, you change the diapers. I'm not doing it."

"And you didn't change her diaper today?"

"Hell, no."

"You're busted. You put the diaper on backwards."

He made a futile attempt to convince me that I had put her last diaper on backwards, but we both knew, and whenever he spoke to his friend Kevin, who's daughter was born right after Trinity, they were like a couple of mother hens clucking over their chicks.

It took a while, but as Trinity grew, she really did grow on Will. The older she got and the more she interacted with us, the more interested he became. The truth is, he never was into the baby thing, but that period doesn't last long. As she was reaching five and six months, smiling and laughing and playing with us, Will became more and more involved with her.

I remember one particular day that was like a revelation him. I was sitting on the couch with the camera, taking pictures of Will and Trinity as he played with her, lifting her up and down, saying, "Up....down....up....down." Trinity was smiling back at him and having a great time, and suddenly Will looked at me and "Hey, you know, this is *way* better than a cat."

"Well, yes," I said.

"I mean, she can learn stuff!"

It wasn't long after that Will decided to teach Trinity American Sign Language. Will had, of course, been reading up on child development, and he'd run across some evidence that a child's brain is developed enough to communicate before they can form words with their mouths. So he went out and got a bunch of books, and managed to teach Trinity to sign a handful of words (no pun intended). She could say things like "milk" and "drink" and "eat" and "more." Will had to abandon his experiment after a while because it had to be a total immersion sort of thing, and Trinity's nanny never got with the program.

Later, as Trinity started to speak and to ask us questions Will asked me to make a promise.

"When I was a kid," he told me, "I would ask my mother questions, like 'Where did the stars come from,' and she'd just make up crap. 'Oh, the angels put the stars in the sky.' I hated that. So let's make a pact."

"Okay, what?"

"No baby talk, and when she asks a question, we answer it. If she asks about an irrigation system, we say, 'That's an irrigation system.'"

We stuck to that, and I still answer Trinity's questions honestly and the best I know how, but, really, I'm a mother, and I couldn't help the baby talk. And if I indulged her with baby talk sometimes, Will indulged her in his own ways, like buying out half a toy store whenever he went into one.

But, still, Will had trouble accepting the idea that he was now just a father like anybody else, or that his feelings for his daughter were just what any father feels. I think there was a part of him that was too cerebral for his own good, and this would be a major example. I don't think that Will could accept that something as simple as creating a child could lead to such profound feelings of real joy.

It think it was the attempt to understand his experience of the unconditional love parents feel for their children, something that doesn't happen on a rational level, that got him into the idea of genetic engineering. Mixed in with it was the cancer scare he'd just had, probably, but whatever combination of events it was, Will came to me one day and announced that he was going to clone himself.

Now, anybody else, you'd have to laugh this off as a joke, but since it was Will, I believed him. He might not have gotten there, but he was going to try. He started reading up in the various fields he'd have to master. We'd go into Coliseum Books up in Columbus Circle, and while I was upstairs looking at novels, he'd be downstairs in the textbook department, and we'd leave with a stack of textbooks on genetic engineering and molecular biology. The two electron microscopes he bought were an indication of how serious he was about this.

I knew that once something challenged him, engaged his mind, he was going to pursue it to the end, or at least until something else caught his attention, so my only request was that he think about cloning the cat first, as a trial run.

Will would have fit right into an age before science had become as professional and academic as it has now, before you needed government funding to take on a big project. He was self-taught, just like all those gentlemen scientists from 200 years ago, and his scientific interests ran in all directions; the narrow specializations scientists work in today would have driven Will crazy if he had to stick to one.

At the same time he was first starting to read into genetic engineering, Will was also researching some other things.

It might have started about a year before this, with a diving trip Will wanted to take, to Bikini Atoll. They'd done nuclear tests there, through the fifties, but now people were diving in the area. There are more sunken WWII battleships there than just about anywhere else in the world, so if you're into that sort of thing it can be pretty interesting. Will had always wanted to go there, and I imagine that's when he ordered all the documents about the tests from the Nuclear Regulatory Commission that had just been declassified, and got the tapes of the explosions to watch.

(By the way, this is the reason Will and I never agreed where Trinity's name came from. He was reading up on Trinity, the first nuclear test, when we went to see *The Matrix*. My sister, Stacey, was with us for the movie, and afterwards, Will and I were going back and forth with names for the baby. His suggestions were along the lines of cells.dot.org', and 'C2465,' while I was coming up with names like Sarah and Jennifer. Stacey said "What about Trinity?" We both liked it. It was a perfect compromise: pretty and feminine enough to satisfy me; unusual and science fiction-y enough to satisfy Will.)

While he was poking around on the internet researching nuclear testing, he ran across something that grabbed his attention. I found out when he asked me "How cool would it be to have your own submarine, Kerry?" He wasn't talking about a little two-person submersible. The Russian navy had decommissioned one of their nuclear subs, and it was for sale. They'd taken all the nuclear equipment off it, and Will got as far as hunting down an ex-Russian navy captain to pilot our sub for us.

I'm sure everyone remembers the big flap over Y2K, and how everyone was afraid civilization would fall apart when all the computers blew up because they couldn't handle a date after 1999. Will was sort of into that, and I guess he thought of the sub as a survivalist sort of thing to do. If things got really bad, he could get his family out.

In the end he didn't buy the sub, but he did prepare for Y2K, and so did his family. Will limited himself to buying MREs from military suppliers on the internet. That's "Meals, Ready to Eat," the current form of military field rations. We had a closet full of them, and despite his gourmet cooking, he insisted they were great. He loved them, and always wanted me to try them, but I never understood the appeal.

As it got closer to New Year's we decided it was time to get out of town. Just in case. Will might have stopped at MREs, but up in Maine, Ralph and Linda were prepared for the revolution. They'd built what we called the Y2K condo, and the whole family was going to be there for New Year's Eve.

Because it was our first year with Trinity, and it wouldn't be fair to leave anybody out, we "did" Christmas three times in twenty-four hours that year. I prepared everyone for our blitzkrieg visits, and so we spent Christmas Eve at my mom's, and then we went to my dad's for Christmas first thing the next morning, and right after, we got in the car and headed up to Maine for Christmas dinner.

When Ralph and Linda had bought the land, there was no house. It had burned down sometime in the past. When we had visited them in the past, they were living in what had been a garage for tractors and other farm equipment. They'd turned it into a pretty nice place, but it was really nothing compared to the Y2K condo. The place must have been something just short of an industrial farm, because the barn on the property was the size of an airline hangar. You could easily line up five cars in there.

Inside, it still looked like a barn, with a loft running along the sides, creating a second floor. They used the space all along there for storage. If you walked all the way down to the end of the loft, to the back wall, there was a barely noticeable knothole in the wood, which turned out to be a plywood door. You slip your finger in and open it, and you're suddenly looking at a beautiful front door, which seemed completely out of context. Open it up and you're in a gorgeous two-story house, all pine paneling and soft gaslight. There was a full bathroom, and a nice kitchen with all the latest equipment, since they were all so into gourmet cooking. Downstairs there was also one bedroom and a living room, and upstairs, there were another four bedrooms, and another bathroom, plus a library.

Out of sight was their own electrical generator. Come the revolution, they were going to be completely self-sufficient. The way it was set up, you could walk all around the barn and never suspect there were living quarters there. There was even a little hidden balcony, if you ever needed to do some sniping.

We stayed there for the week between Christmas and New Year's, and while it was a nice place, and it was great to see the whole family, I was bored stiff. Trinity was four months old, so I was pretty much stuck in the condo with her for my only company most of the time. Linda was off doing her own thing, and Will and Ralph and Bill were out shooting as much as the weather permitted.

I hadn't mentioned that along with motorcycles and gourmet cooking, all the men were very much into guns. It had started when they were all out in Utah so much, getting the restaurant going. Will even got a license to carry a gun. It wasn't valid in New York, but he kept a shotgun around anyway.

I became aware of this one night at around three a.m. I was asleep in the bedroom of our Battery Park City apartment, when I was shocked awake by a loud "BOOM!" I jumped out of bed, thinking the sky was falling, our building was going to collapse or something. I ran into the living room, and there's Will, sitting in a chair with a Grand Marnier in one hand and a shotgun in the other, laughing his ass off.

"Will, are you out of your mind?"

I could see what he'd done. He had the closet door open, and he piled up a stack of pillows and cardboard to absorb the shot. Unfortunately, it hadn't worked. There was a big hole in the closet wall into the bathroom. Thank god the shot had gone right between the porcelain toilet and the porcelain sink. Another two inches and it would have taken out the toilet and we would have had a lot of explaining to do to the owner of the condo (We were subletting.).

"I just wanted to try it, and see what would happen."

"Will, we're on the 22nd floor in downtown Manhattan. Somebody's going to call the police."

"I figure I get one shot. It's the middle of the night. People will wake up, and if they don't hear anything else, they'll go back to sleep."

He was right. He got away with it. It's sort of a scary thought. He could have shot me with a shotgun and nobody would have even called the cops.

Will preferred shooting in a more conventional setting, though, so he had a great time during the week leading up to Y2K, out in the woods working on his marksmanship and doing other woodsy things in case the whole world went Mad Max in the year 2000. In fact, I think I might have been the only one who wasn't disappointed when the apocalypse didn't come on New Year's eve. I was just glad to head back home to Manhattan, where the end was coming, but it wasn't going to be because of Y2K.

That February, we took a trip out to Long Island, to visit our friend Ted. Will had been doing a lot of diving with him, but we'd never visited him at home. This was actually Will's first time out to Long Island, and I'd only been out once, for a weekend, years before. This was the first time either of us had been in Sag Harbor, where Ted lived. It's on the South Fork, on the bay side, and the whole area is beautiful, and it isn't as crowded and trendy as the whole Hamptons scene. We both thought it was really nice out there, and Ted asked, half seriously, if we wanted his father, a realtor, to look around for a house we could buy. Even though we didn't expect anything to come from it, we said, "Sure. Why not?"

We had just about forgotten about it when we got a call from Bill McCoy in March. "I have your house," he said. "You want to come see it?

So we got in the car with Trinity and drove out there. We never looked at another house. We walked in and immediately knew this was the one. Bill said, "You know, I could show you other houses," but we were sure. It had everything we wanted.

The house is on a little hill, away from the main roads, on it's own acre of land, about two blocks from the water. It's a three-bedroom, and after living in apartments for so long, it was huge. There was a fireplace and a pool, and really, everything we wanted. We could both picture us making a life for ourselves there.

So we put in a bid right then, and before we even got back to the main highway for the drive home, the offer had been accepted. We were all set except for the small detail of the mortgage. The problem was that, from the bank's perspective, we didn't look like that good a risk. First of all, they'd rather you didn't own your own business. They think you're more stable if you work for somebody else. But even worse, because of the way the finances were set up, on paper it looked like we didn't make any money. I was okay, but Will's W-2 from the previous year showed something like five thousand dollars.

Will wasn't going to let that stop us, though. He scanned his W-2 in, and made the necessary changes to turn us into likely candidates for a mortgage, and we presented ourselves as employees of Tradeware. The loan came through, and after we got some work done on the place, that was it. We had moved in by June, and from then on, the house in Sag Harbor was home base.

We spent every weekend out there that summer, and we immediately had a cable modem put in, so we could work from there if we wanted to. The only problem, as far as Will was concerned, was the drive. On a good day, we could get out there in under two hours, but going back and forth for the weekends, just like everybody else with a house out that way, we'd end up sitting in traffic for hours. I didn't mind so much, but Will could not accept that from now on, he'd have to give up so many hours of his time to sitting in traffic on the Long Island Expressway.

The solution came to him one day when we were doing exactly that, sitting on the L.I.E. waiting for traffic to start moving again. He was looking out the window, and saw a helicopter zip by overhead. "Now, that guy," he said, "that guy's got the right idea." We were pretty busy, so he didn't get started until the next February, in 2001, but one day announced, "Kerry, I'm going to become a helicopter pilot."

Like everything else he did, he really got into it, and when he started his flying lessons, he stopped even pretending to come into Tradeware anymore. The company was on autopilot, as far as Will was concerned (but, of course, it wasn't; I was there running things, and everybody else was still coming in and doing their jobs), while he was out learning to be fly a helicopter. There's an airport in Islip, a town about forty minutes from our house in Sag Harbor, and he was out there flying pretty much every day. He went though all this training in about half the time people normally do it, and by July, he had his license.

The Downtown Heliport is a short walk from our office, so once he had his license, the plan was to start commuting back and forth. He flew into the city with his instructor a few times, but before he could start doing it on his own, the heliport was shut down. It was September, 2001.

Chapter Ten

"House is broken."

From: kerry@tradeware.com

To: All

Sent: Thursday, September 13, 2001 10:44 AM

Subject: WTC Attack

Hi everyone. Thanks for your concern. We've received so many calls and emails to make sure we were okay that I decided to send this out to everyone at once.

First of all, we are all safe and sound. Here's our story.

We live two blocks south of the World Trade Center, about 200 yards away from the South Tower, and we watched the whole thing from the windows of our 39th floor apartment.

I had just come back from the grocery store with my daughter Trinity, who had turned two in August. Will was still sleeping. Trinity and I were watching TV and waiting for her nanny to come, so that I could leave for our office on Wall Street. I heard a low rumble and a loud blast and looked out the window and saw a huge explosion around the 80th floor of the North tower. I yelled, "Oh my God, Will, look out the window. A bomb just went off in the World Trade Center."

It was hard to believe. We stared out the window, and then turned the tv to the news. Will said, "It's not going to be on the news yet. It just happened," but it was only a few minutes before the news showed up on CNN. I watched in disbelief as the North Tower burned. I started making phone calls, to tell people what was happening right outside my living room window. First I called the office, then my sister, Stacey, who announced the news to everyone in a Starbucks on the Upper West Side, and then my Dad in Boston. I tried my Mom but she wasn't home.

Meanwhile, Will was frantically calling people on his cell phone. CNN was reporting it as a plane crash but Will immediately said that "This is no accident". The West Side highway was closed down right away and we could see all the emergency vehicles and personnel in the street.

I was on the phone with my Dad when there was an explosion in the second tower, lower down, at about the 50th floor. I screamed and said to my Dad "We're getting out of here" and hung up.

We were running around frantically when the phone rang and our receptionist at Tradeware yelled "We're evacuating!" I simply said "Go! So are we," and hung up.

Will had seen first hand the first WTC bombing in 1993, and I think that the whole Y2K thing made a lot of people really think about the problem of getting off Manhattan in the chaos that would follow a disaster, like this one. Will initially said that we were probably better off staying in the apartment rather then dealing with whatever was happening in the streets.

Trinity saw her parents freaking out, so she knew something catastrophic was happening. She was scared and upset, so we took turns holding her, and trying to comfort her. The problem was that she was witnessing the whole horrible scene firsthand. The twin towers were an integral part of our lives; we looked at them everyday, and here they were burning while the news reported other planes being hijacked and showed pictures of the Pentagon after it was hit.

After a while I simply could not look at it anymore. I felt sick to my stomach watching the whole scene. We saw all the fire engines and emergency vehicles converging on the towers below us, but we knew in our hearts that there was really nothing they could do to fight the fires.

After the first tower had been hit, I asked Will, "Is Cantor in there?" Cantor Fitzgerald was one our very first clients when we moved to NYC and we had become friendly wit a lot of people there. I knew the answer, but I wanted him to say no. Somehow, I thought, that could change it. But we saw the gaping hole high up in the center on the North Tower. That was where the elevators and stairwells were located, and we knew that anyone above that was not going to get out.

I was sitting on the couch watching the devastating news reports, trying not to look out the window, when I started hearing weird sounds. I asked Will what it was. He didn't know, but he was looking at the towers through a spotting scope. After a minute he groaned, then said, "Oh my god, you don't want to know..."

It was the sound of people jumping from the towers.

It was so horrible to sit there with that awful realization, knowing that each time we heard that sound, it meant that somebody's life had just come to an unimaginable end.

We were still trying to figure out our best course of action when we suddenly became aware that our own lives were in serious danger.

I was in the living room with Trinity when Will screamed in terror from the other room. "Oh my god! Its falling!" I looked out the window and saw the scariest thing I've ever seen in my life. I watched in disbelief as the South Tower began a slow, horrible descent to the ground.

I grabbed Trinity and ran to the center of our apartment, where there are no windows, because I thought that would be safest. Will was in the bedroom, and leaped out into the hall with us. We just stared at each other in shock as we tried to brace ourselves for whatever was going to happen next.

From the hall, I could see through the bedroom window, and I watched the South Tower collapse in what seemed like slow motion. The was a deep rumble, truly frightening, that we could feel as well as hear. I could hardly believe I was seeing with my own eyes. I thought about how many times I had looked up at the towers and tried to calculate if they would hit us if they fell, and here it was actually happening. The ground shook and I tried to process the understanding that we were on the 39th floor and the building might very well collapse underneath us.

I thought that the huge mass of the towers falling would be like a huge bomb going off, and take out anything standing in the area. I was convinced our building was going to collapse. I stayed, crouching against the wall with Trinity, until the terrible rumbling stopped. I was still waiting for the windows to blow in or the floor to start to go, but to our amazement, nothing happened.

We decided we'd better leave, and ran out of the apartment and headed down 39 flights of stairs; Will and I took turns carrying Trinity. All the people going down the stairs did their best to stay calm, keep moving, and just get down to the lobby.

As we got to the lower levels the dust that had started to fill the air we were breathing immediately got worse and we knew there was no place to go to. Everyone huddled in the lobby and the building staff gave out painting masks for us to breathe through. There weren't that many people there, because so many people were at work.

Outside, it was as if a nuclear bomb had gone off. A cloud of debris right outside the glass entrance made it as dark as night. We still had electricity but then someone yelled out that the second tower was falling. We all listened to the second rumble, the lights went out, and then it got even darker outside. I have to admit that I felt a small sense of relief that they were both down, and my fear of immediate danger subsided a little. I kept remembering the earthquake during the World Series in California and the gas explosions that followed, but I did feel that probability that we were going to be okay had greatly improved.

Will, Trinity and I huddled on the floor in a corner by the mailboxes, as far away from the lobby windows as we could get. We waited there for hours while the dust and debris settled. Eventually, emergency workers came and announced that there was a full evacuation order. The whole area was being evacuated and locked down. They were going floor by floor in every building to make sure everyone was out, and then locking down the buildings behind them. We were all supposed to head a few blocks south to the very tip of Manhattan where there were boats ready to ferry everyone to NJ.

Everyone else was leaving, but we realized we had nothing with us, including some medications Will needed, so we made a short list of supplies and he proceeded to climb back up the 39 flights of stairs. Up in the apartment, he ripped open a fifty pound bag of cat food and left it on the floor for our 3 cats, along with many bowls of water. He gathered diapers, bananas, shoes for Trinity, his meds and some water for us, and started back down the stairs.

Downstairs, I insisted that I wasn't leaving until my husband came back down, which left me and Trinity alone in the lobby with the building crew and the emergency worker. Everyone else was gone.

It seemed like Will was gone for a long time, and I was worried about him, but he finally came back. We put on masks and went outside and headed south to the boats. There was a foot of dust and debris on the ground, and the only people we saw were police and emergency rescue workers. I think I now know what it would be like if a nuclear bomb went off. What had started out as a beautiful sunny fall day had turned into something out of a science fiction disaster movie.

Our original plan had been to skip the boats, and instead head to the Brooklyn Bridge and walk over it. It was just too hot though, and I couldn't make it that far carrying 32 lbs of little girl.

I was so thankful that at least it had happened while we were still all together in the apartment. I don't know what I would have done if I had been in the office, with Will and Trinity at home. Trinity's nanny called right before the first tower collapsed, and she had been on West St., which is the northernmost street of the WTC complex. We feared for her life. (Later that day, we found out that she was okay.)

We got to Battery Park, the southern tip of Manhattan. People had gathered there to evacuate, or to help with the evacuation, and everyone was offering us food and water and gas masks, especially for the baby, and urging us to get on a boat. Most of the boats were headed to New Jersey, and we wanted to get to our house on Long Island. Since every available commercial and private boat was lined up ready to take people, we decided there had to be a boat going to Brooklyn which would take us in the right direction.

We finally found a large red tug boat and got on. As we pulled away from the shoreline I looked up and saw the huge dust cloud. The wind was blowing all the dust and debris over toward Wall St and Brooklyn. Every once in a while the wind would make a clearing in the dust and it was bizarre and unreal to see the empty area in the skyline where the World Trade Center had been just a few hours earlier.

We got to Brooklyn and started walking, and I realized that a friend of ours lived in the area. We found her apartment and she was home. We immediately opened turned on the news, and started trying to plan how to get out of the city. We were really concerned that they might lock down the entire city, or worse, that there might have been biological weapons, like anthrax, used in the attack. We wanted to get as far away as possible.

Nicole, the girlfriend of Cody, one of our sales reps, called Will's cell phone looking for him. She was freaking out because she hadn't heard anything from Cody. She had a car so we decided to all bug out of the city and get to our house in Sag Harbor.

Well, we made it our to the house by 7:00PM and heard from Cody. We immediately started trying to relax and calm down. I was so happy to be out and away from it.

Trinity woke up screaming last night, and when she saw the pictures on TV of what she considered her home, she simply said, "House is broken." I guess that just about sums it up.

Cantor Fitzgerald, a major client, had their offices and a huge trading floor on the top floors (103-106) on the north tower (the one that got hit first). We know there is no one left and there is no way any of them got out. We keep the servers for their systems in XXXX, and they were untouched by the attack. It was spooky and surreal to find that it was all still up and running, like a ghost of the company.

My guess is that it is going to take years to clean up the devastation and they will never build anything there again except a memorial. Also, I'm guessing all the buildings immediately surrounding the WTC complex will have to be torn down. We are hoping that our building is intact, simply so we get our cats, and also things like passports and birth certificates, but I don't think I could every live there again. I will always worry that the building sustained structural damage and might collapse.

That's our story. Believe me, every single person that was in downtown Manhattan that day will have been traumatized by a similar experience. As someone who lived through it, and saw the whole thing, I know that thousands of people perished that hour. Over the next few months we are all going to find out we knew many people that died that day.

y

Chapter 11

The Best Days and the Last Days

Just like everyone else in New York, it was a long time before things felt normal to us again. Everyone in the country, really. We didn't even know what normal was supposed to be after that. It was such an abrupt and shocking event that forever after everybody will always think of there being a "before" and an "after"; you don't even have to say before or after what.

For me, though, it was also something else. For me, 9/11 was also the opening scene of the last act, a marker for the beginning of a rush of events that can at times all blur together in my mind, and at others stand out as a series of discrete moments of happiness and frustration, like beads of different colors on a string. Some of them, anybody would be grateful to get a few days like that in a lifetime, and I am, but they don't exist out of context, the memories are tangled together in the year they all had to be squeezed into. And, in the end, it was more than anything else the year that my heart was ripped out of me and my world fell apart.

For the rest of September, I sort of holed up in the house. We never did live in that apartment again. Will went back and got our things when residents were allowed back into the area, and, eventually, when everything had settled down, Cody and Nicole moved into the apartment, so I was in it again, but I never spent another night there.

We moved ourselves completely to Sag Harbor and it was a while before I started to come back into work regularly. Coincidentally, we had been in the process of moving Tradeware into larger offices in September. We'd taken a floor in the Trump Building at 40 Wall Street. Everything was put on hold for a while, but we got a call from the rental agents at the end of that week, and they asked us if we still wanted the space. We did, of course. Life goes on. We ended up being the first commercial lease signed on Wall Street following 9/11.

Will was in the city a lot more than I was, and I wasn't seeing as much of him. But even before 9/11, really, I remember feeling really lonely, because it was so seldom Will did anything with me and Trinity. There were the flying lessons, and when he was home, he was always hovering over electronics, or working on something else. He was really getting into genetic engineering at that point, and he'd developed an interest in building an atomic clock, too. He ran into too many brick walls on that project, though, so he bought one to take apart to understand them better, and then another, and then he just went ahead and spent $80,000 on a really nice one to keep in the office at Tradeware.

I was happy for him, and glad he was enjoying his projects, but the occasions when we did things together were so rare that they stand out for me. I really wanted him to participate more with Trinity. Not just for me, not just because I was lonely, but because he was missing it: our daughter was growing up. She would never be two again, and she would never get to be with her father when she was two again.

I have pictures of the day that we all went to Pumpkin Town that October. It's a farm out in Southampton where you go into the fields and pick your own pumpkins for Halloween. With all of us doing something out in the fresh air and sunshine together, having a great time, I clearly remember thinking "This is as good as it gets." It was one of the first times since 9/11 that I could just focus on where I was and who I was with, and Will was as present as I was. I was thinking that this was the best day of my life, but it felt like more than an observation. It felt like a premonition.

The same thing had happened the previous Christmas.

The Christmas when we'd done all that traveling, trying to visit three families in two days, we'd ended up fighting a lot, and agreed that we didn't want to do that again. This year, we'd already been up to Maine for Thanksgiving, so we were going to stay home for Christmas. If anyone wanted to see Trinity (our ace in the hole when it came to visiting), this year they could come to Sag Harbor.

It was really pretty wonderful. We did all the Christmas-y things you do, and we were excited about our first real Christmas tree. I remember that Will had just brought it home and got it set up in the stand. He had gone into the kitchen and Trinity was in the living room with me, and I had started decorating the tree. I was in the middle of hanging the ornaments when I was suddenly slammed with the realization that this was the last Christmas that we would have together. The feeling was so strong that it literally stunned me.

My first thought was Trinity, that something was going to happen to our baby, because that's how mothers think. I ran to Will and told him what had happened, because if anyone knew premonitions and visions and messages from other planes, it was Will. This time, though, he was sure I was wrong. He insisted that I didn't have to worry about it, that nothing was going to happen to Trinity. He was right about that part.

By the time the last guest had left and the last turkey sandwich was eaten, I had forgotten all about it.

Will had been out shooting again when we were in Maine for Thanksgiving, and once we were home, he mentioned that his back was bothering him. We assumed he'd twisted it, or hurt himself with the recoil while he was shooting, or something like that, and Will decided to see if it didn't just get better.

Right after New Year's Cody and Nicole came out to visit for the weekend. Will cooked for everybody, but as soon as dinner was served, he disappeared. We had dinner, expecting him to come back any minute, and when he didn't, I went to look for him. I found him in the bedroom, in so much pain he had to go lie down. That night was one of the few times I can think of that he went to bed at the same time.

At three in the morning, he woke me up to tell me that he was going to the emergency room. I said I'd drive him; since Cody and Nicole were there, it would be okay to leave Trinity. He insisted on driving himself, though.

When he got back the next morning, he had some painkillers, but they couldn't say what was wrong with his back. That began three months of pain, pain pills, and doctor's visits, until he finally got an MRI in March, which revealed a slipped disc. They had tried various medications, but none of them were working. At one point, early in the process, when they had him on some kind of nerve drugs, Will got very upset because his arm was going numb, and it was freaking him out. So, one of the first things he did was go to a chiropractor, hoping to relieve the pain and fix whatever was wrong with his arm. Oddly enough, of all the specialists he saw, that chiropractor was the only one who diagnosed him correctly. He looked him over and said, "I'm not touching you. You've got a slipped disc."

Will didn't like the drugs they gave him at first. I was afraid at one point that he was going to become addicted to Vicodin, but it gave him terrible nightmares, and he asked the doctors to put him on something else. In Will's terms the nightmares were more than just bad dreams. Vicodin opened the door to evil spirits; it interrupted his defenses in the dream plane, and invited them in to screw with him. The doctors switched his drugs a number of times, and I think what he ended up taking most was just Valium. I say "just," because it seems like such a minor thing, but Valium is highly addictive too, and I think Will might have been taking it until the end. On top of that, I know that Will was afraid he was developing a drinking problem. He'd never mentioned it to me, but he'd discussed it with Ralph.

So, to say that the whole experience was really awful is almost an understatement, but the thing that bothered Will about it most is something else completely. After he had the slipped disc, the next time he was measured, he'd lost an inch. He'd been 6'1", and now he was 6' even. He hated that!

Finally, after he got the MRI, the doctor gave Will a neck brace to wear, and it helped a lot. He wore it full time for about a week, and used it on and off after that. It relieved his pain, but he never got that inch back.

Will always wanted to surprise me on my birthday with something outrageous. Every year he tried to come up with something that outdid all the birthdays that came before it, like the time he completely filled my office with flowers. I was never so surprised, though, as I was on my 39th birthday, when Will asked me to marry him.

I had always wanted us to get married, but to be honest, I'd kind of given up on it by then. By that point in our lives, we had become partners in every way a man and woman could. We were always together; even if we were not physically in the same room, we were each conscious of the other, and remained in the same place emotionally. We were best friends, lovers, business partners, parents and playmates. My mother used to say to me, "How do you guys do it? I don't know anyone that spends more time together then you two."

What more was there? What could getting married add to that? As Will would say, marriage was just a convention of society, and our relationship existed outside of the context of some traditional outdated formality. Besides, I had already been married, so that made it less pressing for me. To tell the truth, I was just grateful he had gone along with fatherhood.

So, I never pressured Will on marriage, never even brought it up. I had convinced myself that it didn't matter. In the end, though, it was really what I always wanted, even if I had talked myself into believing it wasn't. Almost.

I think the combination of his cancer and 9/11 had a lot to do with why he finally proposed. When you're looking at the possibility of final things, even if you keep your intellectual distance from the ways of the world, those sentimental conventions can take on a lot of significance. And, possibly, though I didn't think about it at the time at all, he was being practical, anticipating a time when Trinity and I would have to get by without him. If we had never gotten married, there would be innumerable legal hassles to confront at a time when we were least able to cope with them.

Of course, when he asked, he didn't bring up any of that, and I feel pretty safe assuming that he wasn't thinking about it at that point, either.

My birthday, November 1, fell on a Saturday fell on a Saturday, and we were out at Sag Harbor for the weekend. My sister Stacey was visiting, and we all went out to a nice restaurant for dinner, something we didn't usually do because we always had Trinity with us. She was just then getting old enough to come with us.

Later that night, at home, Will and I were in bed, and he just said, "Well? Will you?"

I knew what he meant right away, but I checked to make sure.

"Are you asking me what I think you're asking me?"

"Yeah. So, will you?"

"Of course I will," I told him.

The word "marry" never came up.

It wasn't until the next morning that I thought to ask, "Aren't I supposed to get a ring or something?" I didn't want to make a big deal of it, though, so when Will said he'd get around to it, I didn't think about it again until Thanksgiving. It was the first time I was seeing most of our family since my birthday, so that's when everybody found I we were getting married. It turned out to be sort of embarrassing, because every time I said we were engaged, somebody would say, "Where's the ring?"

So, with Christmas approaching, and the ring something he still hadn't gotten around to, I did start bugging Will. I wasn't going through another big family holiday without a ring on my finger. But it got down to the day before Christmas, and still no ring. So, when Will called on Christmas Eve--he had to go into the office that morning--to say he was on his way home to Sag Harbor, I told him not to bother coming home unless he has an engagement ring with him.

Will and Cody told me later what happened. After he hung up the phone, Will roped Cody into going up to Tiffany's with him. They called a car, and headed uptown from Wall Street. They were talking about what kind of ring Will should get in the back seat, and it must have been really obvious that Will hadn't looked into this at all and didn't know what he was doing. The driver, whose son had just gotten engaged, interrupted them. He said he could help if they'd hold on a minute, and he pulled the car over. In the trunk were a bunch of books and guides his son had used to research gems and rings; he got them and out and Will and Cody crammed until they got to Tiffany's. Will ran in just as they were closing, and even though he hadn't planned ahead and didn't have any time to shop, he managed to pick out a beautiful ring.

It was beautiful enough that when he finally walked in the door, handed it to me, and said, "Here, asshole," I didn't mind.

We set the date for June 1, 2002, which fell on a Saturday. We were going to have a huge reception on June 9th at the Four Seasons, and we'd put so much time into planning that event that we hadn't put any thought into the actual marriage ceremony itself. We had arranged for our friend Ted's father, Bill McCoy, the same man who found and sold us our house, to come at three to perform the ceremony. In addition to being a realtor, he was also a justice of the peace.

Earlier that week, on Monday, we had gone to the Southampton Town Hall to apply for a marriage license. We thought we could just walk in there and get one, no problem at all, but of course it's always a mistake to make plans assuming that there won't be any problem. The Town Clerk politely turned us down.

Will needed to bring in an original birth certificate, and I needed the original decree of divorce from the court in

Massachusetts. There was really no reason to panic yet, but I couldn't help indulge in a little bit of freaking out. We got home and hit the phones. I called my mom, who graciously volunteered to drive to the Dedham courthouse, where my divorce was processed, and FedEx the divorce decree to me in Sag Harbor.

Will's birth certificate wasn't so easy to get our hands on. The hospital in Detroit where he was born no longer existed. (For a while it looked like, technically, neither did he.) After many phone calls, though, Will finally waded through the various state and city bureaucracies to track down the proper office to obtain his records. He finally reached the right person at 12:55 in the afternoon on Wednesday. The civil servant in charge informed him that she had his records right there. Will said, "GREAT! Here's my FedEx account number. Could you send them overnight, please?"

"I'm sorry, but we close at 1:00 pm on Wednesdays. You'll have to call back tomorrow."

"But it's not 1:00 yet! Can't you please get it out today?"

"I'm sorry, sir. We close at 1:00. Please call back tomorrow, and I'll be happy to send it."

"*But I'm getting married on Saturday!* We have to get the certificate before that. Please, could you do it today?"

"I'm sorry, sir, but it's now 1:00. This office is closed."

Click.

The Sag Harbor Town Hall closed at 4:00 on Friday. The birth certificate was going to be sent who-knew-when on Thursday. More freaking out ensued, and it must have helped, because you'll be glad to know that it all worked out and we left town hall on Friday afternoon with a marriage license.

That night, while Cody and Will hung out in the backyard, discussing whatever it is two men discuss when one of them is about to get married, Trinity, my sister Stacey, Nicole, and I watched *Cinderella*, the original animated Disney film. Through some quirk of circumstance, I had never seen it before, and it was the perfect movie to see for the first time the night before your wedding.

I woke up the next morning to a perfect summer day. After sunning by the pool for a while, Stacey and I decided to go to the Starbucks in Bridgehampton to get some coffee. We brought Trinity with us. After we'd gotten lattes for us, and milk and a donut for Trinity, we found a table to sit at.

"So, you never told me what you're going to wear for the ceremony," Stacey said.

"I have no idea." I'd never really thought about it, and now that I did, I realized that I didn't have anything appropriate. "I don't really have anything."

I think that saying that so calmly was what made Stacey stare at me as if I were insane.

"Okay, that's just crazy," she said. "You have to wear something special when you get married. There's a little vintage clothing store down the street. Let's check it out."

I was now becoming kind of worried about what I would wear, so we took our coffees and went to the store. As soon as we walked in we spotted a white dress that would be perfect for me. I asked to try it on and the woman working there took it off the mannequin for me.

I went into the dressing room and discovered that it was just a tiny bit too tight. I came out and asked to see it in a larger size.

"I'm sorry," the woman said. "That's the only we have. I can try to get it for you in a larger size. When do you need it by?"

"Three o'clock? For my, um, wedding?"

It took her a minute to absorb the fact that I was getting married in a few hours and had just started looking for a dress, but when it sunk in, she said, "You know, there's a lingerie shop right next door. The dress comes so close to fitting you, maybe if you put on a bodysuit under it, it would work perfectly." She went next door and got one for me, and then picked out shoes a string of faux pearls and a set of matching earrings. Everything looked great. The whole ensemble worked perfectly.

We left the store about an hour after we walked in, carrying my wedding dress, shoes, accessories and one feminine secret, all for $125.00. I couldn't have had a more perfect outfit if I had planned for months and paid a fortune.

We got back in the car, and it was actually getting to be late enough that time was becoming an issue. Stacey decided to push it. "You know," she said, "How about some flowers?"

I spotted a florist right down the street. "If you watch Trinity," I said, as I drove down the block and parked again, "I'll run in and have them make me up a bouquet."

I ran in and explained the situation to the florist. "You seem awfully calm for someone who's getting married in two hours." He laughed, and then proceeded to create a lovely bouquet for me and a smaller but equally beautiful bouquet for Trinity, who was of course very excited about being the flower girl.

By the time I got back to the car and we headed home it was almost 2:00, but we'd managed to whip up a great little wedding on a moment's notice in a couple of hours. The ceremony went perfectly, except for one thing. I discovered afterward that I had worn my wonderful wedding dress backwards.

If the wedding in the backyard was the perfect pastoral scene, a ceremony on summer day with a handful of the people we were closest to, the reception at the Four Seasons a week later was the complete opposite, but it was perfect, too.

Will had planned everything. He picked out the entire menu, he planned the decorations, he picked out all the flowers. He wanted to make this the most amazing party anyone had ever seen, and if it wasn't, he must have come very close. It was a wonderful party, and not at all traditional.

One of the best known rooms at the Four Seasons is the Pool Room. It was designed by Philip Johnson and Mies Van Der Rohe, which is about as good an architectural pedigree as you can get. The focus of the room is the white marble pool at its center, but due to drought conditions in New York in the summer of 2002, it was going to be empty the day of our reception. Will was not one to be defeated that easily though, and proposed to the restaurant's management that they fill the pool with Perrier. Unfortunately, word got back to Mayor Bloomberg's office, this being his crowd and all, and he told the restaurant that he'd have them closed down if we did that. I guess he didn't want us setting a frivolous example in the face of a drought. Instead, Will had the pool filled with flowers, which was even better.

It was a great party, and everyone we knew was there. My whole family, the entire extended Marino clan, was there, and besides the members of Will's family I already knew, like Ralph and Bill and Linda, a lot of people came that I'd never met before. It was the first time I met his mother and his sister, who he didn't have a lot of contact with.

We had a great band, and the dancing got really wild, with everybody out on the dance floor. Neither Will nor I are really dancers, and we were sort of pathetic. Will had come up with a plan , but a little too late to put into action. We were going to take dance lessons, and practice and practice until we had learned to perform one dance so perfectly that we looked like professionals. We'd get up there for the first dance, dazzle everyone, and then stay off the dance floor, so they'd all think we could do that all the time. Instead, we danced clumsily, but had a great time, and even if I was a little embarrassed, the pictures from the wedding make us look like we know what we're doing.

We left for our honeymoon the next day.

When we were deciding where to go, Will was all set to take another island trip. We'd never made it to Bora Bora together, and that was somewhere we'd talked about from the time we first met, so Will wanted to honeymoon there.

I wanted to do something different. We'd been to Mauna Lani Bay, and Saba, and I really didn't want to get on a plane for 26 hours to go to the other side of the world. To be honest, with 9/11 less than a year before, I was still afraid of flying. I could do it, but not without a sense of dread, and I didn't want it to last any longer than it had to.

I had never been to Europe, though, and I thought that would be fun. Will was reluctant, but I insisted. We always go scuba diving, I told him. Let's just do something different this time. Finally, he agreed, and we booked a two and a half week trip, starting in Rome. Like so many other things Will was initially reluctant about, once we got there, he ended up loving it.

What turned him around was his realization, as soon as we arrived, that he'd been in Rome before. Will had always talked about his past lives, and we'd figured out that we had been married in a previous incarnation, but I've never seen him so gripped by a past-life memory as he was in Rome. "I've been here, before, Kerry. I lived here when the Romans were still here."

I loved it, too. I'd be happy living there. I had a fantasy of getting an apartment there, and just moving. It was that beautiful.

We did a lot of the usual things you do in Rome, but the morning after we arrived, when we got up, Will's first response to the city of Rome was "Screw the ruins. Let's go shopping." And we did. There were a few times on that trip when I felt like Julia Roberts in *Pretty Woman*, when she finally went into a Rodeo Drive store with a proper introduction. Shopping at Armani in Rome was like that. Will was good at many things, but I have to say, nobody was better than Will at spending money.

In between shopping expeditions, we did find time to see the ruins and some of the other usual tourist sights. Will liked the Circus Maximus best. He said it didn't feel dead like the other ruins.

Other places, I had to drag him to. For instance, he really, really didn't want to go to the Vatican. It was the last place he wanted to go in the world just about. I virtually had to beg. And when we walked into St. Peter's Cathedral, he didn't react to the beauty of the art and architecture; he saw past it. His first comment was, "Oh my god! What an incredible amount of money this must have cost." A tour-guide had told us that there secret escape passages built in all over the Vatican for the pope. After he'd seen St. Peter's, Will said, "No wonder the pope needs secret escape routes." He thought the whole thing was an unbelievably ostentatious display of wealth on the part of the Catholic Church, and a really bad idea, politically.

Basically, Will thought the entire Vatican was in bad taste.

We both appreciated the less spectacular sights and places in Rome more. We had some great meals there, and the best ones were at little places that weren't in the guide books. One night, we were in a little piazza, and found a great little family restaurant, and sat down for dinner. We did what we always do. We just said, "Feed us!" We always got the best meals that way. We let them decide what we were eating, and of course, they outdid themselves bringing us their best dishes. The food was amazing.

We sat and drank some more wine after dinner, and then I said, "Come on, let's walk back to the hotel."

Will insisted we'd get lost, and wanted to take a cab.

"If we get lost, we'll ask someone. There are people everywhere. Come on. I want to see the Trevi Fountain. It's on the way, and it's supposed to be beautiful, especially at night. We can walk by it."

The Trevi Fountain is probably the most famous fountain in the world. Even people who have never been in Italy know it from seeing it *La Dolce Vita,* and *Three Coins in the Fountain,* and it was one of the things I didn't want to miss while I was there.

Will walked with me, but he was bitching and moaning all the way. "You're going to get us lost, Kerry. Let's just find a cab."

We *were* a little lost by then, but there was a little old Italian man sitting on the corner, and I asked him where the Trevi Fountain was.

He pointed and said, "Right down the street."

We kept walking and then, all of sudden, there it was.

Will immediately said, "Oh my god, that's amazing!"

And it was. It was beautiful. The Trevi Fountain consists of an incredibly lifelike scene out of Roman mythology, with Neptune standing upon the rocks and winged horses emerging from the sea, and surrounding them and behind them friezes and statues of other mythological figures. It's almost impossible to take it in all at once, but however close you can get, it's breathtaking.

We joined the throng of people in the plaza in front of the fountain and gaped like, well, tourists.

If you want to come back to Rome, the old superstition says you have to face away from the fountain and throw a coin in, over your left shoulder. So I said, "Will, give me some change," since he was carrying all our money.

He didn't have any, so I never threw a coin in the fountain, and now he'll never be back to Rome. With the memories I have of being there with Will, I don't know if I will either.

It was a great trip, but it wasn't all great. There were clouds hovering over our honeymoon, too. There was a big U.N. function while we were there and everyone was on a high terrorism alert; helicopters constantly buzzed by overhead. But weighing on us more heavily was being separated from our daughter. We were both really edgy about being so far away from Trinity. We hadn't expected to feel this way. We knew we'd miss her, but we didn't realize it would interfere with our trip. My mother was staying with her in Sag Harbor, so we knew everything was alright, but this was the longest we'd been away from her since she was born, and we just didn't like it. We decided then that we'd never take a trip without her again, or at least not for a long time, until she was much older.

We weren't ready to call off the rest of the trip yet, though, so after two nights in Rome, we set off for Sardinia, where he had reservations at what was supposed to be the best hotel on the island. But as soon as we got there, we picked up the nastiest vibe.

Sardinia's an odd place to start with. Because it's in a strategic spot in the Mediterranean, different countries have been fighting over it for a couple of thousand years. It's mostly been under the control of different powers that we think of as part of Italy, and has been since the 18th century, but from around the 14th to the 18th century, it was ruled by the kingdom of Aragon, which became part of Spain, so there's a strange mix of cultures. It's like the Spanish version of Italy.

It's a physically beautiful place, and we stayed at a five-diamond resort, but we were both uncomfortable from the minute we landed. We couldn't figure it out, but Will and I had the same response: "Ew. Get us out of here!"

On the shuttle from the airport, everything seemed sort of weird. There wasn't much going on, and there was a flat feeling to everything. Then, when we checked into the hotel, at around three in the afternoon, there was just nobody there. It was like the Overlook from *The Shining*. You would have thought we were the only guests in the whole place.

Our room didn't make us feel any better. It was just a normal room, nothing special, but at a resort like that, you expect more, and we were pretty disappointed. I started feeling claustrophobic almost as soon as we got into the room, too. So, the first thing we did was go down to the bar to get a couple of drinks. I was pretty hungry and asked the bartender if we could get a sandwich or something, and he explained that there was no food service available until 5:30.

This was a hugely expensive, five-diamond resort, and there was no food available anywhere in the hotel until 5:30. This made no sense at all. Will and I shared a bowl of peanuts at the bar, and waited for dinner. It wasn't until later that we found out that we had arrived on the day of the

World Cup, and all the other guests were in their rooms watching the game. Probably a lot of the staff were off doing the same thing, too, which explained why everything was so deserted.

Even so, the vibe was weird, and we were on the phone with our travel agent that evening. "Get us the hell out of here!" we told her.

We had originally wanted to go to Capri, but at the time she booked the trip, she couldn't find us anything. Now she did, though, and she arranged for us to go there, but we had to stay where we were for two nights. We figured we could handle anything for two nights, so that was all right.

On the second day, we decided to check out the town; maybe it was just the hotel and not the whole island making us so uncomfortable.

It was a nice, picturesque fishing village. Okay, we thought. Nothing wrong here. We had dinner at a little restaurant, and that was perfectly pleasant, too. ("Feed us!" works as well in Sardinia as it does in Rome.) This was the trip we'd been hoping to take. We didn't want to go back to the hotel at all, but it was getting late, so we headed back. We weren't ready to go to our room, though, so we asked someone if there was another place in the hotel to get a drink.

We were directed across a little moat with a footbridge. We headed that way and it took us into a part of the hotel we hadn't been in before. Everything we saw there was gorgeous. The bar was in a beautiful room, and when we used the bathrooms in the lobby, we both came out saying how amazing they were. That was the first time I really understood what people were talking about when they say "Italian tile."

We asked some of the staff some questions, and that's when we figured it out. We were now in the original hotel, the one that had gotten such a great reputation. At some point, there had been an an expansion, and the new parts of the hotel, where we were staying, were a pale imitation of the original. It had none of the history or substance, and definitely none of the beauty. It was just a copy of the authentic thing, and we could feel it as soon as we got there.

Whether that's what caused the bad vibe where we were, or whether the expansion was just built on a spot with bad power lines, we had no way of knowing, but Will and I did some experimenting, walking back and forth across the footbridge, and there was a definite line where things changed. The energy was as different as night and day.

There were only eight rooms available in the original hotel, and that was why we'd gotten booked into the new part. We called up our travel agent, who must have thought we were crazy, and explained that we weren't. Then we told her which rooms she should always ask for in the future.

We went on to Capri the next day, and that was everything we'd hoped it would be, with some more serious shopping, but, really, for most of the trip, we just wanted to get back to Trinity.

The next trip we took was for her. At the end of October, coming up on my birthday, we took Trinity for her first visit to Disney World. She loved it, of course. She was actually a bit scared of all the big Disney characters in their costumes, but she still thought it was the best place she'd ever been. We did all the usual things: Minnie's house; It's A Small World, all the different rides. I had a great time taking her all over the place, but the times I enjoyed the most were when Will came with us.

It was up and down with Will during the trip. There was a bad sign I chose to overlook when we first got there. We were staying in the Polynesian Hotel, and downstairs in the lobby is a little store. The first thing Will did after we checked in was go down to the store and stock up on liquor. He filled the mini-fridge with those little bottles you get on airplanes.

Will hung out with me and Trinity about half the time on that trip. We got a babysitter one night, and went out to dinner, but most of the time, Will was just as happy staying back in the room sipping from the bottles, smoking, reading, and working on Tradeware stuff. In fact, on the day we left, Will decided to stay at the hotel while Trinity and I went back out to the Magic Kingdom for a last visit. When I got back to the hotel, Will showed me a some notes he'd made. He had spent the morning brainstorming a software architecture that became our newest product, MarketTrader, a real-time market data display system. It was all done on Polynesian Resort stationary, which made it kind of funny.

Will hadn't shown much interest in Tradeware for some time, and he seemed to be experiencing a new surge of energy that might have been some kind of turning point for him. He'd been through a long period where he was turning away from things, and I think this might have been the moment when he started turning back.

I'd seen it during another moment on that trip. It was the day we all went to Epcot. There's an exhibit there with a series of fountains where the jets of water are choreographed, like the fountains in Las Vegas. They almost looked like a living thing, as the arcs jumped from one place to another, like a big worm, and Will was fascinated by them. He started timing the pulses of water, trying to figure out the formulas they were using to create the impressions they did. He got down on his knees to peer into one of the fountains, and got taken by surprise by a jet of water in the face. I have a picture of that moment. Trinity is laughing, and so is Will, and we were all having the best time.

That was the last time I thought it. "This is the best day of my life. It doesn't get any better than this." It was almost scary, how certain that felt.

Chapter 12

The Last Act

Will had always enjoyed his toys, and since we got the house, he had added luxury cars to the list. When we'd met, Will had no credit, because of the unfortunate incident when he'd abandoned a car on the side of the road, and then defaulted on the payments. After that, during his time with Rama, he was living off the grid, so it wasn't even that he had bad credit, it was that there were no records of him for a stretch of years. No credit makes the lenders even more uncomfortable than bad credit.

So, to build up his credit rating, Will had convinced me to cosign a lease for a new car after we moved to New York. We got a Jeep Grand Cherokee (top of the line for Will, of course), and for three years, that was our car.

Now though, we were both driving more, and the lease was up, so Will got us a Mercedes sedan, the S430. After three months of driving that in the Hamptons, though, Will had noticed that a lot of people were driving a better model than we were, so he traded in our Mercedes for an S600, the top of the line. It was a pretty expensive upgrade, and there aren't that many of them around. Will said that the only people that notice the 600 are people driving 500s, and I have to admit that it was fun to pass some snooty Hamptonite in his Mercedes and know that he was envying ours.

The 600 became my car, because Will next got himself a Porsche, a black '97 Turbo Carrera. But then, all of a sudden, right before we went to Disney World, he showed up in the driveway with a second Porsche. It was a beautiful car, there was no denying that, but it looked exactly the same as the first one to me. Will told me that this was THE car, though. It was a Turbo S, and there were only around 20 made.

We also had a van that Will used for his cave diving trips with Ted, and a Mercedes G Wagon, the Mercedes SUV. As soon as Mercedes announced they were going to be producing these, Will put us on the waiting list. We got the third one from the dealership in the Hamptons. (Christie Brinkley got the first and Dick Grasso, at the time Chairman of the Stock Exchange, got the second.)

By fall of 2002, we had five cars, four of them seriously expensive, and it had become a problem. The insurance company kept canceling our policies, because they were convinced that, with five cars and two drivers, we were pulling some kind of insurance scam.

It was just Will's impulse buying, though. When he saw something he wanted, he got it. He never stopped to check the price, or to see if he could get a bargain somewhere else. In fact, it was right around then, in October, that he drove up to the house on a weekend when Stacey was visiting and walked in the door with a big plasma screen tv. It wasn't even in a box. He told us it was a floor model and he'd gotten a great deal on it, and Stacey and I gave him a hard time about how that was the first time he'd gotten a deal in his life. Saving money just wasn't something Will he thought about, and really, at this point, it wasn't as if Trinity was going to go without anything because Will got a new toy.

So, once he got his helicopter license, it was a pretty safe bet that he was going to buy himself a helicopter.

Through the end of that summer and into that fall, Will was spending most of his time in Sag Harbor. I know now, from others, that his drinking was probably getting out of hand, enough that Will was starting to worry about it. He was still taking the pills he'd started in on because of his neck injury, even though his neck was much better. He had even, I found out recently, bought cocaine once or twice.

Emotionally, he'd become more withdrawn, and we hadn't been getting along as well as we used to. I was going into the office regularly, or taking care of Tradeware business from home, while Will was pursuing his own projects in our basement-- genetic research, atomic clock experiments, diving stuff--and flying his helicopter.

Will found the helicopter he wanted to buy on the internet, a military surplus Gazelle, being sold by the British Royal Navy. The Gazelle is one of the fastest helicopters ever built, and it's widely used by both the British and U.S. armed forces. There was a lot of paperwork involved, but it was finally delivered in August. He was still going up with his instructor, though, because despite having his license, he still needed specific lessons for the Gazelle before it would be safe for him to fly it solo.

We got back from Disney World on Monday, and my fortieth birthday was that Friday, November 1. Will told me he had a surprise for my birthday, but he wouldn't tell me what it was. He finally gave in and told me that we were going somewhere, and that we were leaving on Thursday morning. Thursday was Halloween, though, and although Trinity had a costume the year before, and we saw a little pre-Halloween party at Disney World, this was probably the first Halloween Trinity was going to really appreciate. Besides, we'd gotten her a genuine Disney Cinderella costume at Disney World, and Trinity couldn't wait to show it off to everybody. No way were we going to miss that.

Will agreed to reschedule for one week later, but he still wouldn't tell me where we were going. I really didn't want to do anymore flying. I still couldn't help thinking of 9/11 whenever I contemplated getting on a plane. I could do it, and I did, but I really preferred not to. We'd been to Europe for our honeymoon just a few months before, and getting on a plane for a six or eight hour flight to spend the weekend in Fiji, say, was the last thing I wanted to do.

What I was really hoping for was a romantic weekend at the Gurney Inn, a great spa in Montauk, out on the tip of the south fork of Long Island. We had gone a few times for massages, and I had loved it. We never stayed overnight, though, and it seemed like it would be a wonderfully intimate and romantic way to spend the weekend.

In the middle of the week I was just outside of Will's office and overheard a phone call. He was saying that he wasn't going to be available for something next week because he'd be in Europe. It was not what I wanted hear. I didn't let Will know I'd overheard him, but I reminded him that I wanted to do something close to home for my birthday. He told me not to worry, but I was pretty sure at that point that I was going to have to go to Europe, despite all his attempt to keep all his plans a mystery.

We still hadn't decided what to do on Friday, the actual day of my birthday. Will had asked me what I wanted to do a few times, but I'd been in a bad mood most of the week because of my suspicions about what Will was planning and my fear of getting on a plane, and I'd told him every time that I didn't care. Will went ahead and made arrangements on his own. He reserved the chef's table at Alain Ducasse for dinner, and asked my sister

Stacey and our friend Peter, who runs our favorite restaurant, Bayard's, to join us.

On Friday morning, the day of my birthday, I was sitting at my desk, and Will came into my office and announced that he had a surprise for me. He was followed by what seemed like an endless procession of delivery men carrying roses. For about ten minutes, they kept coming in, leaving roses and going back out for more. Will had gotten me forty dozen roses. "One rose for each month of your life," he said. Because that wasn't excessive enough, I guess, he ordered half a dozen other arrangements to go with them.

My office smelled like heaven and looked like something out of a musical from the forties. For then, at least, I forgot what I had been in such a bad mood about, and appreciated how Will felt about me. It was like the roses surrounded me with his love.

I didn't get much work done the rest of that day. The only problem was that it was Friday, so I'd have only one day to appreciate the roses, and they'd be wilting by the time I saw them again. I told Will, "It's too bad my birthday wasn't on a Monday, so I could have enjoyed them all week."

"That's not the point," he said. "The point is just to enjoy them now."

At 5:30, Will told me that the car was waiting for us downstairs, so we got Stacey, who'd been working at Tradeware for a while at that point, and went downstairs. We picked up Peter and headed up to midtown.

Alain Ducasse probably isn't the most expensive restaurant in New York; I think it's only second or third. Even so, it's undeniably the most luxurious and decadent restaurant in New York. The restaurant itself is beautiful, with a sense of luxury so intense that it's like it seeps out of the artwork and glittering crystal and shining silver into the air, and you breathe it in as soon as you step through the door. But even that wasn't enough for Will. It might be one of the most beautiful restaurants we'd ever seen, but there were private rooms that were even better, and Will had reserved the best one for us.

The chef's table is in a room that gives you a clear view through a window of the chefs at work. The other walls are all mirrored, so that whichever way you looked, you could see into the kitchen. The ceiling had tiny embedded lights, and they were reflected in the mirrored walls, too, so it looked like the night sky was twinkling above, and you were dining under the stars. The setting was really extraordinary.

LIFE"S TOO SHORT TO DRINK CHEAP WINE

The waiter entered the room, and announced that we were about to experience something very special.

Will ordered a bottle of wine, and then, instead of us all looking at menus, Will said, the way he always liked to, "Feed us!"

The waiter asked if we like mushrooms. Everybody at the table did. The chef had gotten some unusually good porcini mushrooms that day, and we were soon eating course after course of exquisite dishes, each one with porcini mushrooms in it. Everything was accompanied by fine wines chosen by Will and Peter, who is a serious wine expert. Even after dinner, when we were all so full we thought we couldn't consume another thing, and we'd already had a bottle of port, they ordered one more bottle of the wine I liked best, Chenin Blanc. The wines that night were just that good.

We were there all night, and I think we were the last to leave. The rest of the restaurant was empty. On the way out, they handed me and Stacey elegant little bags, each one containing a piece of the white porcelain fruit we had admired in the lobby and a delicious breakfast cake prepared by the pastry chef for the next morning.

After we had dropped Peter and Stacey off, I couldn't resist asking Will how much it all cost.

"Guess," he said, and laughed.

"I have no idea," I told him, but proceeded to guess anyway. I knew it was expensive, but no matter what I said, he kept saying "Higher."

He finally told me that dinner had cost $11,000. I couldn't believe it. My jaw dropped.

"Will, that's insane!"

"You only turn forty once, Kerry. Might as well enjoy it."

And I did, very much. But $11,000, that's a small business loan, not a dinner bill.

Although we'd moved home base to Sag Harbor, and I never went back to our old apartment in Battery Park City, we had taken a new apartment there after everything had settled down a bit. We'd stay there during the week when we were working, and if we'd been out late or we'd both been drinking, it was a real convenience to have a place right there. Our plan was to be living out in Sag Harbor during the week within the next year or so, so Trinity could start school there.

For now, though, we still had the apartment, and that's where we woke up Saturday morning after my birthday, hung over. When my head cleared a bit, I drove out to Long Island with Trinity, and Will followed a little later. We were already in the habit of driving two cars because Will was always driving back and forth from the house to the airport to fly the helicopter.

We stayed out at the house until Wednesday. I worked from home, and Will was at the airport a lot, having work done on the helicopter. On Wednesday, we came back into the city for a wine tasting Will had scheduled for Tradeware employees that night. We wanted them to know how to order a bottle of wine when they were out with Tradeware clients, bit it wasn't really business; it was lots of fun, too, a treat for all of us.

Trinity's nanny, Naomi, was staying at the apartment with us, so it was okay that we didn't come home until one or two am, pretty drunk again.

When we got into the bedroom, Will pulled out a suitcase and told me to pack. The trip I'd been dreading was scheduled for the next morning. I didn't know what to pack, though, because Will still hadn't told me where we were going. I'd been asking him for two weeks, and it was still a secret.

"How can I pack when you won't tell me where I'm going?" I asked him, and we ended up having a huge fight. He was making me crazy, and to be honest, by this point, I wasn't cooperating. I couldn't be less enthusiastic about going on this trip, and it didn't help that we were both drunk. The fight was bad enough that I ended up sleeping in Trinity's room that night, something I'd never done before. Since Naomi was in the trundle bed, I slept on the floor.

In the morning, very early, I heard the alarm going off, and went back into our bedroom. I tried to wake Will up, but he was out cold, and I still didn't want to go on this trip, so the truth is, I didn't try all that hard. I hit the snooze button, got into bed, and went back to sleep. I must have hit it a couple of more times, because the next thing I knew it was 7:00. I shook Will, and this time he got up.

As soon as he saw the time, he jumped out of bed.

"God damn it! You fucking bitch. Did you change the alarm?" he said, and we were instantly fighting again.

"I tried to wake you, but you wouldn't get up."

"Well, get packed and let's go. We have a fucking plane to catch!"

"I still don't know what to pack, because you still haven't told me where we're going!"

"Fine!" he yelled. "Here, asshole!" and he threw the itinerary to the ground. "This is what you fucked up. Now pack, because we're going to make this plane!"

We had reservations for the Concorde to Paris from JFK at 8:00 am. Will had made reservations for the chef's table at Alain Ducasse in Paris that night, and then he was going to take me on a shopping spree.

Will had called for a car and we were out the door by a quarter after.

"We're going to make this plane," Will insisted.

We fought all the way to the airport. I was hung over and unhappy, but I wasn't terrified anymore, because I knew by point that there was no way we were going to make it.

Still, despite everything, the driver got us to the AirFrance terminal by 7:50. We ran up to the counter, and said we were on the 8 o'clock flight. The guy working there didn't quite laugh at us, but he might as well have. Sorry, he said. You're a bit too late. There was nothing we could do.

We took a cab home, alternating between fighting and not talking to each other the whole time.

When we got home, I crawled right back into bed. I was exhausted and still feeling sick from last night. I know Will was, too, so I was surprised when he told me that he was going in to the office. I was planning to drive back out to Sag Harbor later in the day, and asked Will to stay home and come with us. I knew as well as anyone that Will wasn't in the office often, and never early in the day, so this was pretty unusual.

He insisted he wanted to work that day, though. I know that he'd been getting all fired up about MarketTrader, the new product we were going to create based on the work he'd done at Disney World, but I think that he really just wanted to get away from me for a while. There wasn't anything I could do about it, so he left for the office and I went back to sleep.

A little while later, I was woken up by the phone. It was Will, and he'd called to apologize. I apologized, too. I asked him to come home, but there was one more piece of business he wanted to get to, and he needed me to help him take care of it. Just like Will had to have the Mercedes 600 because everyone else had the 500, Will had his heart set on getting an American Express Black Card. Amex only gives the Black Card to its best, highest-rated customers, and it's by invitation only. There's no spending limit, and it comes with all sorts of privileges. They maintain a staff of people just to take care of things that people with Black Cards want, like getting hard-to-find goods, or access to things that are usually off limits. It's like a credit card that comes with a concierge.

Ever since he'd heard about the Black Card, Will had wanted one. Will had hoped to be a millionaire by now, and despite our success with Tradeware, I think he was pretty disappointed that he hadn't reached his goal, but he could at least do this. Because I was the primary cardholder on our corporate account, they had to talk to me. Will called back in a little while and we did a conference call with American Express and he got his Black Card.

By one o'clock, I had Trinity packed up and we drove out to Long Island. The house in Sag Harbor was my refuge, and it was a huge relief to get there. I couldn't wait for Will to join us. I was looking forward to making up and spending a quiet family weekend together. I expected him to show up that evening, after work, but when we talked later in the day he told me he wouldn't be driving out until tomorrow. Trinity and I were both disappointed, but at least we'd have the rest of the weekend.

In the morning, we had a staff meeting by videoconference, and after it was over and everyone else had left the room, I asked Will when he was planning to come home. It was a Friday, and if he left at 5, he'd be in traffic for hours, so he agreed to leave as soon as he'd taken care of a few things. He told me he was thinking about flying.

I'd heard the weather report and it wasn't good. "Will, do not fly," I told him. "There are 30 knot winds."

Besides, it just wasn't practical. The helicopter was at the airport in Islip, and he'd have to drive an hour to get that far. Then, after a ten minute flight to the East Hampton airport, I'd have to drive out and pick him up, anyway.

"Okay," he said. "I just have a few things to do, and then I'll leave."

I spent the day with Trinity, having lunch at a place with an old-fashioned soda fountain, then going to the park. Really, I was just killing time until Will got home. We hadn't actually seen each other since the big fight Thursday morning, and I was starting to feel a lot of anxiety. I just wanted us to make up and move on.

I got home with Trinity around five or six, when Will should have been well on his way out to Sag Harbor. I hadn't heard from him since that morning, though, and I had one of those horrible thoughts you have when somebody you love is late. *What if something had happened to him?* I knew I was being ridiculous, though, so I tried to push those thoughts out of my head.

Eventually, I made dinner for Trinity and later put her to bed. I made a fire, had a drink. Hours passed, and Will still hadn't gotten home, or even called. I didn't want to bug him, so I put off calling, but finally, at 8:30 or so, long after he should have been home, I called his cell phone.

"Hello!"

"Will, where are you?"

"I'm at Cody's place, Kerry. His parents are in town, so we're all over here hanging out." He sounded like this was perfectly reasonable, and it was too bad I couldn't join him. I blew up.

"Fuck you, Will, you asshole! You were supposed to come home yesterday! I've been waiting for you for two days! Now you're going to get drunk and you're not even going to be here until tomorrow! Just, fuck you."

I hung up on him. I was so upset I threw the phone across the room. It shattered into a hundred pieces. I could not remember ever having been this upset and depressed before. Would my husband really go to these lengths just to avoid being with me, or was he just being a jerk?

I was so tired and miserable that I finally just crawled into bed, at around 9:30. I was no longer expecting to see Will that night, but at 10:00, right after I'd put my book down and shut out the light, the phone rang.

"Hey. What are you doing?"

"What do you think I'm doing? I'm sleeping. I've been waiting for you for two days, and now I'm sleeping. Where are you?"

"I'm just getting to Exit 50…. Are you going to wait up for me?"

Exit 50 on the Long Island Expressway is at least an hour away from us.

"Hell, no, Will. You're not going to be here until 11 and I'm exhausted. I'll see you in the morning." I hung up, and eventually, I fell asleep.

Trinity woke me up around seven. She slept in our bed almost every night, and if Will got home after the two of us were asleep, he'd usually crash on the couch downstairs, or in the guest bedroom, to avoid disturbing us. So, when Trinity asked me to get up and make her strawberry milk, I told her to go downstairs and wake up Daddy, and ask him to do it. I thought this was pretty funny, because Will is not a morning person, and I was getting back at him a little bit.

"But Daddy's not here," Trinity said. There was something in the way she said it that terrified me. Why wasn't Will here? And how did Trinity know?

"What do you mean he's not here?" I asked her.

She gave me a funny look, and repeated herself. "Daddy's not here."

I bolted out of bed and ran downstairs, and immediately began to panic. There was no good reason for Will not to be here. He'd called me from only an hour away last night.

I called the Southampton police, and said that my husband was missing. I told the woman that took the call that he'd been at exit 50 on the LIE last night in a black Porsche around 10. Had there been any accidents? I asked her. She wasn't helpful at all; she was actually pretty rude, as if I were bothering her when she had much more important things to do. She didn't know if there'd been an accident, she told me, and no, she had no way of finding out. She suggested I start calling every hospital between Exit 50 and my house.

I didn't even know where to begin. I only knew one hospital, Southampton Hospital, and I couldn't figure out how to find all the other ones and get their phone numbers. I calmed myself enough to make Trinity some breakfast, and while I was doing that, I had a horrible thought. *What if…*

But, no, Will wouldn't have taken up the helicopter at 10 pm in bad weather, when I wasn't even going to be awake to pick him up at airport. That made no sense.

I picked up the phone and called the hangar anyway, almost as a way of avoiding the task of finding and calling all the hospitals. Peter, Will's flight instructor, answered the phone.

"Peter, it's Kerry Smithers. Is Will's helicopter there? He didn't get home last night, and I'm worried about him."

"I don't know," he said. "I'll go check and call you back."

Somehow, I started to know the answer, and I was going crazy waiting for the phone to ring. It took him about five minutes, but it seemed like an hour.

"Kerry, the helicopter's gone and his car is here."

It felt like my heart had fallen out of my chest.

"What do we do, Pete? What should I do? We were fighting. I don't know where he went!"

Pete asked if he should start a search.

I didn't know. Maybe Will had decided at the last minute to fly up to Maine because he was mad at me. He could have gone anywhere. I called Maine, and they hadn't heard from him. I called Pete back and told him to start the search.

When I called Ted and told him, he was here in ten minutes. He did his best to calm me down and distract me, but I was freaking out.

Pete called back. He'd found Will's flight plan. He'd left at 11:06 heading to East Hampton. There was no mistake. Will had gone up in the helicopter and wasn't heard from again. He was missing. Pete notified the FAA and the Coast Guard and the search began in earnest.

Ted and I started making phone calls. Ralph was on a plane to Salk Lake City, but we reached Bill, and he was waiting for Ralph when he got off the plane. They got the first flight back to New York. Linda started driving down from Boston; Cody, Stacey, my parents; everyone headed out to the house.

We tried to protect Trinity, but she could tell something was wrong. People started pouring into the house, and before long we could hear the search going on. You could hear the planes and helicopters flying low, looking for wreckage. Cody and Ted went out to help searching, combing the shore for anything that might have turned up.

It wasn't until late after ten o'clock that night that I heard anything from the Coast Guard. The whole day, listening to the search, waiting for the phone to ring, knowing that at any time somebody might have some information, I was jumping out of my skin. I waited and waited, anxious and scared. Finally, after Trinity had fallen asleep and I'd gone upstairs to put her to bed, the phone rang. Somebody called me from downstairs to pick it up. It was Commander Nelson of the Coast Guard.

He started telling me about the search and rescue operation, going through everything they'd done, step by step, and it took all the self-control I had left to listen to the details. There had been 10 foot seas and 30 mph winds, with a nor'easter coming in. *I knew that! Why wouldn't he tell me if they found Will?* He went on and on, and it seemed like forever before he said that they'd found some wreckage washed up on shore, and it had been positively identified as Will's helicopter.

I didn't faint, or scream, but I knew in my heart that was it. I started crying then, and everyone in the room, all our family and friends, could tell what I'd just heard.

Will was gone. Our adventure was over.

Epilogue

In Dreams

It wasn't until a week later that I started coming out of my initial shock. There'd been announcements and legal matters to deal with at Tradeware, where I was now the unprepared CEO; there'd been all the people calling who knew and loved Will; finally, on Friday, a week after he died, there was the celebration of Will's life—not a wake, a celebration—at Bayard's, and an amazing number of people had shown up. It had lasted until two in the morning. The whole week till then had been a blur.

On Saturday I woke up at the apartment, and people started coming by to say goodbye, as family and friends headed home and I prepared to drive back out to Sag Harbor. All the stress and emotion had taken its toll on me; I was a wreck. There was so much pain in my shoulders from holding myself tight that I couldn't get myself a glass of water without wincing, and if I did, I wasn't coherent enough to remember where I put it down.

When Ralph and Linda came by, Linda said, "Come on into the bedroom. You can take your shirt off and I'll give you a back rub." Everybody else stayed in the living room while Linda took me inside and massaged my shoulders. I hadn't realized until then how desperately I need that.

Linda talked to me gently, telling me that she'd been reading from the Tibetan Book of the Dead every day, the traditional rite to help the soul move on to the next plane. It was what Will would have wanted. I took comfort from that, and as I began to relax a little, I started talking.

I thought I would have had trouble sleeping, I told her, but that wasn't true at all. I was sleeping so solidly that it was more like going under general anesthesia: I'd put my head down on the pillow and the next thing I knew, I'd wake up and it was morning. "Linda," I said, "I'm not dreaming. I always dream. Big, vivid dreams that I remember the next morning."

"Kerry, that makes complete sense. You need energy to dream, and you have none. Give yourself a break. You're not dreaming because you've been in shock and have no energy. Just relax and you'll heal yourself."

A little later that day, after everyone had gone, and Trinity had been to a dance class—I was trying to keep some normality in her life, and wanted her to go on rehearsing for a dance recital she was going to be in—I got in the car with Trinity and Stacey and we headed out to Sag Harbor.

Stacey drove, and we got there by 7 o'clock. It felt so good to be home. It was the first time since Will died that I hadn't been surrounded by people. We watched some television together, and had a glass of wine. Trinity fell asleep and I put her to bed, and only a little while later, around eight or nine, I went to bed myself, exhausted.

I fell instantly asleep, and immediately had a dream, except it didn't feel like a dream. It felt more like a visit. It was real. Will had come to me, and there was nothing else he could have said that would have left me so at peace with everything that had passed.

I walked into a smoky bar and there he was, standing at the bar. I knew it was weird, because I knew he was dead, but we looked at each other for a moment, and then we hugged, and it felt so good. We hugged for what seemed like a long time. And then he looked me in the eyes and said, "I'm satisfied."

"Are you alone?" I asked him.

He chuckled and said, "No, Kerry. There are lots of people here."

And then I woke up.

The End

from alt.zen

Jun 18 1994, 5:12 pm

I need some guidance from the Taoists out there. I am a thirty-one-year-old man living in Chicago, and I have begun to sense that I must somehow detach myself from the madness that is today's society. I feel that I need more solitude, more quiet, perhaps a teacher.

I have been to a Zen monastery in upstate NY near Woodstock, but I could not help feeling out of place. The people I found there were looking for the feeling of enlightenment and not the thing itself; they seemed to need a religion.

Is my distinction understood? Please, someone point the way. Do not lecture! POINT!

Okay, Jim. You are being honest, it seems. I hate that. Having taken Buddhist vows, I am bound by dharmic duty to reply as honestly as I personally can when someone asks an earnest question about self-discovery. The rest of the time, I can pretty much goof off and tell people whatever I think will piss them off (hey, it's a hobby). If I am really having a good day, I can both tell the truth as I see it AND piss people off. So, that said, here's my .0000002 cents. Don't spend it all in one place.

I agree with you about "feel-good" enlightenment vs. the real thing. For me, personally, the feel-good thing is self-dishonesty. Of course, I can only say this because I did the feel-good thing for many years. There is a place for it, and I completely respect all people who follow any path that may lead them to personal happiness. But it no longer works for me. What I find *does* work is really learning how to meditate—how to cut to the core of consciousness and find the worlds of perfect light. In short, how to collapse the world by stopping thought, and thereby gain a silent mind. Everything else seems to lead me to sheer tortured misery.

So go find yourself a teacher you personally like. Shop around. Be very careful. In my experience, many spiritual groups in the U.S. have really nice wrapping paper, and that's all you can see at first. Do your best to cut through this and see the core of what they are really doing. If you like what you see, stay awhile. If not, move on. IMHO, the only valid indicator of how much a teacher will help you to learn to meditate is how well they meditate themselves. A lot of spiritual trappings and a big focus on other things besides meditation is a good indicator that they are not really that into meditation. Good meditators are usually extremely well-grounded and very, very funny. If they are not funny, how could they possibly be really detached from the illusion of self?

A big kiss-ass hierarchy is usually another warning sign. If you can't get direct access to the big cheese without more than a little effort, I have found it usually isn't worth the trouble. Also, look at the teacher's students for an indicator of the teacher him/herself. If they strike you as a bunch of spacey flakes, the teacher is either extremely tolerant and these are newbies, or he isn't very effective in teaching them how to meditate. Do the older students lay a power trip on newbies, and if so, does the teacher let them get away with it? Do they seem to have it a lot more "together" mentally and spiritually, and humor-wise than the younger students?

In other words, look for a track record—look for results. Meditate with the teacher. Once you get a little practice under your belt, you should notice a marked difference in your meditations when the teacher is also meditating. Then again, you may not; that's a tricky one. Finally, look for results in yourself. Your meditations should make you happier, more or less, every day. Again, this is only my personal formula; it may not work for you at all. We are all different, and all walk different paths. Hopefully they lead to the same place in the end. Happy Hunting!

-Will Smithers

The American

Buddhist Society

"We now return you to our regularly scheduled program of blasphemy and outrageousness"

ABOUT THE AUTHOR

Kerry Smithers sold Tradeware Corporation on Dec 31, 2009. She now resides in Park City, UT with her daughter Trinity.